CW01083585

WHEN THE FIRES BURN HIGH
and
THE WIND IS FROM THE NORTH

The Pastoral Science Fiction of Clifford D. Simak

by

Robert J. Ewald

A Thaddeus Dikty Book

The Borgo Press

An Imprint of Wildside Press LLC

MMVI

The Milford Series
Popular Writers of Today
ISSN 0163-2469
Volume Seventy-Three

ISBN 1-55742-217-6 (hardcover)
ISBN 1-55742-218-4 (paperback)

www.wildsidepress.com

FIRST EDITION

CONTENTS

DEDICATION

To Donna,
Who made this a labor of love

PREFACE

In his long career, Cliff Simak was virtually ignored by critics in America except for Thomas D. Clareson, and was pigeonholed as a Midwest pastoralist. Roald Tweet says that Simak deserved this assessment because of a "paucity of ideas"—he is a writer who tended "a small plot and tended it well, growing the flowers he knows best."[1] When I first began this study in 1978, having only read *City* and *Way Station*, I might have shared that opinion. However, after reading and studying Simak intensely for the last twenty-six years, corresponding with him and sharing this study with him before his death, I find this narrow stereotype a misrepresentation of the breadth and sweep of Simak's ideas. He always chafed at efforts of fans and critics to restrict the science-fiction genre, and his skill at reducing cosmic events into homey and folksy terms often fooled people into missing the intelligence and wisdom of his writing.

This study may help to dispel the pastoral stereotype and show that Simak pursued a variety of themes in his work and that this variety was apparent early in his career. The chapter on the early Simak reveals that the seeds of his later works can be found in his earlier stories, often dismissed as pulp hackwork. I have organized the rest of the book based on this chronological framework, for Simak seems to have developed as a writer in tune with changes in American society. As a lifelong journalist, Simak was always sensitive to events and changes in American life, and his fiction reflects that sensitivity at various stages of his career.

One critical opinion I agree with wholeheartedly is that Simak was a moralist who wanted to prick humanity's conscience but always with a sharp stiletto, not a blunt sword.

5

To two special people I owe the completion of this first book: to my patient, long-suffering wife Donna, who for seven long years has given up vacations, evenings, and weekends, to the word processor—and to that grand old man, Cliff Simak, who contributed his considerable moral support and wisdom whenever I asked him.

And also a very special thanks to Muriel Becker, whose bibliography and encouragement made this task much less arduous, and to the late Tom Clareson, without whose insights this study might never have begun.

—Robert J. Ewald

A CLIFFORD D. SIMAK CHRONOLOGY

1904 Clifford Donald Simak is born on August 3 at Millville, Wisconsin, son of John L. Simak and Margaret Olivia Wiseman.

1910 (through 1929) Simak attends a country school to the eighth grade, graduates from Patch Grove High School, takes a one-year teacher's training course, and spends several years teaching rural school. He tries to work his way through the University of Wisconsin, but run out of funds.

1929 Simak and Agnes (Kay) Kuchenberg are married (April 13). Only a few weeks earlier, Simak accepts a position on the *Iron River Reporter* (Michigan) where he remains until 1932.

1930 Simak submits his first story, "The Cubes of Ganymede," to *Amazing Stories*. T. O'Conor Sloane accepts it, but returns the manuscript two years later.

1931 Simak publishes his first story, "The World of the Red Sun," in the December issue of *Wonder Stories*.

1932 Simak publishes his first story in *Astounding Stories*—"Hellhounds of the Cosmos." Simak is employed by the *Spencer Reporter* (Iowa).

1934 Simak works on the *Dickinson Press* (North Dakota).

1935 Simak goes to work for the McGiffin Newspaper Company and is given a number of editorial assign-

7

ments in Spencer, Iowa; Excelsior Springs, Missouri; and in Worthington and Brainerd, Minnesota.

1938 After a five-year dry spell, Simak starts writing science fiction again for *Astounding* under Campbell's editorship.

1939 Simak is employed as a copy reader on the *Minneapolis Star and Tribune*. His first novel, *The Cosmic Engineers*, is serialized in three parts in *Astounding* beginning with the February 1939 issue.

1940 Simak becomes Chief of the Copy Desk at the *Minneapolis Star and Tribune*.

1944 Simak begins the *City* series in *Astounding* with the May issue.

1947 Simak's first child, Richard Scott, is born.

1949 Simak is promoted to News Editor on the *Minneapolis Star*.

1950 Simak leads off the first issue of *Galaxy* with his second novel, *Time and Again*.

1951 Simak's daughter Ellen is born. With much reluctance, Simak rewrites Campbell's potboiler, *Empire*, for the Galaxy Science Fiction Novel Series.

1952 Gnome Press publishes *City*, Simak's first hardcover book. *City* has rarely been out of print since. *Ring Around the Sun* begins a three-part serialization in the December issue of *Galaxy*.

1953 *City* wins the International Fantasy Award for Fiction.

1958 Simak cops his first Hugo for Best Novelette with *The Big Front Yard*.

1959 Simak becomes Editor and Coordinator of the *Minneapolis Tribune* Science Reading Series. Simak wins the Headliner award for editing a yearlong study quiz, "*Minneapolis Star* Program of Information on World Affairs."

1960 Simon and Schuster publishes the first hardcover anthology of the many short stories Simak wrote during the fifties, *The Worlds of Clifford Simak*. Simak begins a weekly column in the *Minneapolis Star*, "Tomorrow's World: Science in the News."

1961 Simak launches an ill-starred theatrical career when his short story "How-2" is made into a play, *How to Make a Man*. The play closes in New York after a short run. A four-part serialization of *Time Is the Simplest Thing* as *The Fisherman* begins in the April issue of *Astounding*.

1962 Another anthology of Simak's short stories, *All the Traps of Earth and Other Stories*, is published by Doubleday in the U.S. and simultaneously by Four Square Books in London. Simak also publishes a novel that did not see magazine publication first, *They Walked Like Men*. *Time Is the Simplest Thing* is Hugo runner-up for Best Novel.

1963 *Here Gather the Stars*, later called *Way Station*, begins a two-part serialization in the June *Galaxy*. Simak's Science Reading Series in the *Minneapolis Tribune* wins Best Idea of the Year Educational Award for a newspaper used in the schools.

1964 *Way Station* wins Simak's second Hugo for Best Novel.

1965 *All Flesh Is Grass* is Nebula Runner-Up for Best Novel.

1966 Simak wins the Westinghouse Award from the American Association for the Advancement of Science for his Science Reading Series in the *Tribune*.

1967 A third anthology of Simak's short stories, *Best Science Fiction Stories of Clifford D. Simak*, is published in London. Simak publishes two novels, *The Werewolf Principle* and *Why Call Them Back from Heaven?*, both in hardcover. In non-fiction, The Minnesota Academy of Science Award goes to Simak for his Science Reading Series.

1968 Simak returns to magazine publication with *The Goblin Reservation*, a three-part serialization beginning in the April *Galaxy*. The novel is Hugo Runner-Up for Best Novel.

1969 Simak begins a weekly column, "Medical Report," in the *Minneapolis Tribune* and becomes Feature Writer for the Sunday edition of the *Tribune*.

1970 Simak publishes another so-called "zany" novel, *Out of Their Minds*. Simak's novella, "The Thing in the Stone," is the Nebula Runner-Up for Best Novella.

1971 Simak is Guest of Honor at Noreascon, the 29th World Science Fiction Convention, where "The Thing in the Stone" is nominated for the Hugo Award. *Destiny Doll* is printed in the Spring *Worlds of Fantasy* as *Reality Doll*. Simak edits the 1971 *Nebula Award Stories*, his only anthology.

1972 Simak again publishes two novels, *A Choice of Gods* in hardcover, and *Cemetery World*, which begins a three-part serialization in the November *Analog*. Simak's short story, "The Autumn Land," is nominated for the Hugo Award.

1973 Simak becomes a member of First Fandom and receives a retrospective Nebula for *The Big Front Yard*.

Our Children's Children begins as a two-part serial in the June issue of *Worlds of If.*

1974 Simak's much overlooked novella, "The Marathon Photograph," is included in *Threads of Time*, a collection of three novellas edited by Robert Silverberg. Simak's "Construction Shack" is nominated for the Hugo Award.

1975 Simak's fourth collection of short stories with an introduction by the author, *The Best of Clifford D. Simak*, is published in London. Simak breaks into the fantasy market with *The Enchanted Pilgrimage.*

1976 After forty-seven years as a newspaperman, Simak retires in August to devote himself to more writing, and *Shakespeare's Planet* appears.

1977 Simak is awarded the Grand Master Award by the Science Fiction Writers of America, only the third writer to receive such an honor. Simak's fifth collection of short stories, *Skirmish: The Great Short Fiction of Clifford D. Simak*, is published, spanning his career from the forties to the seventies, and Simak publishes his twentieth novel, *A Heritage of Stars.*

1978 Simak receives the Jupiter award from the Instructors of Higher Education for *A Heritage of Stars.* Simak publishes two hardcover novels—his second fantasy, *The Fellowship of the Talisman*, and *Mastodonia.*

1979 Simak returns to the magazines when his novel *The Visitors* is serialized in three parts beginning with the October issue of *Analog.*

1981 Simak is Guest of Honor at the Denver Worldcon. *Project Pope* is nominated for Best Novel, but Simak wins the Hugo and the Nebula for Best Short Story for "Grotto of the Dancing Deer."

1982 Simak publishes two hardcover novels, the fantasy story, *Where the Evil Dwells*, and *Special Deliverance*.

1983 Simak stops writing science fiction because of illness for the first time since 1938.

1985 Simak's beloved wife, Kay, dies December 7.

1986 Simak publishes his twenty-seventh and final novel, *Highway of Eternity*, at age 82.

1988 Simak dies April 25 at age 83 in Riverside Medical Center in Minneapolis of complications caused by emphysema and leukemia.

I.

LIFE AND CAREER

Clifford D. Simak belonged to that very select group of writers over seventy-five whose well of creativity never dried up and who looked like they would continue to write forever. Unlike his fellow Grand Masters Robert A. Heinlein and Jack Williamson, who had long fallow spells, Simak, until his illness in 1983, had been producing at the rate of at least one novel per year for more than twenty years. Although his short story output had been considerably reduced over the final ten years—short stories not paying nearly as much as novels—there seemed to be no decrease in the quality of his award-winning work. As late as 1981, Simak garnered the Hugo Award for Best Short Story with "Grotto of the Dancing Deer" (*Analog*, April 1980), and his novel *Project Pope* was nominated for the 1982 Hugo.

Over his long career, Simak never had trouble adjusting to the changes in magazine science fiction since he was first published in *Wonder Stories* in 1931. He responded to the demands of every major editor in a wide variety of styles, while still retaining his uniqueness. As Frederik Pohl aptly describes his versatility, Simak wrote "Gernsback gadget fiction, *Thrilling Wonder* space opera, Campbell Golden Age thought-variants, Gold-*Galaxy* satire, and *F&SF* New Wave free style," and lately, he had added neo-Tolkien fantasy to his list of credits. His influence on younger writers was enormous; many freely acknowledge their debt to him. In the appreciations written for a Special Commemorative Issue of *The Creator* on his fiftieth anniversary as a writer, Isaac Asimov credited Simak for his own "plain" writing style, admitting Simak was his prose model, while Frederik Pohl eulogized his consistency, and Robert A. Heinlein envied Simak his discipline.

Simak's discipline as a writer was no small accomplishment. Except for the last years since his retirement in 1976, Simak had always been a spare-time writer. For forty-seven of his fifty-seven years as a science-fiction writer, he was a full-time newspaperman and successfully combined fiction and journalism, two often diametrically opposed careers. Simak "scribbled" whenever he could find time, even if for only fifteen minutes before dinner, and tried to write every day, a habit formed from early childhood and a compelling desire to be a writer.

To the point of cliché, Simak had been tagged by many critics as the "pastoralist" or "regionalist" of science fiction, probably because of the tremendous popularity of *City* with its emphasis on the flight from the cities to the countryside. But a more likely reason is that Simak set many of his stories in small towns, usually in Millville, the name of the Wisconsin town where he was born. He peopled his tales with small-town characters—handymen, drunken bums, village idiots, farmers, and local newspapermen. Into this quiet, bucolic atmosphere, Simak would thrust an alien visitor or a world catastrophe, or one of his bumpkins would develop a psychic talent. If the main portion of the story were set elsewhere, the protagonist often returned to Millville even from the far reaches of the galaxy for a final conflict.

Kingsley Amis was the first critic to label Simak as the "science fiction poet laureate of the countryside."[1] Simak confessed that he had exaggerated and idealized the region where he was born so much that he virtually exiled himself from his own homeland. In a taped interview with Thomas D. Clareson, Simak declared, "For many years, I would visit the folks and relatives two or three times a year, but later I would drive around and find I was disappointed in the real country. I'm very careful not to go back...I don't want to spoil the country I've imagined...."

In Simak's fiction, this return to the countryside is almost a moral imperative if humanity is to survive. In story after story, Simak pits plain horse sense and hick-town shrewdness against the greed of urban sophistication. Big business coupled with technology and their stepchild, the over-organized society of the cities, has brought humanity to the brink of self-destruction and created a moral vacuum. Only a revival of those frontier values still present among certain men who have either remained in the country or moved back to the country can save humankind from itself.

Simak conveyed this moral seriousness in a simple, feeling prose style, lightly laced with ironic humor. Simak's yarns are sprinkled with homely Midwest dialect like "hunker" or "naked as a jaybird." Perhaps it is this quasi-Mark Twain ambience that accounts for Simak's appeal to British critics, for the British seem to have been much quicker to recognize Simak's talent and to write full-length critical appraisals of his works.

This American quality, or more appropriately Midwestern American quality, undoubtedly is a reflection of Simak's early life.[2] Growing up on his Grandfather Wiseman's farm in southwestern Wisconsin, Simak hunted, fished, swam in a creek in the summer, and tobogganed and ice-skated in the winter. The ancestral farm sits on a high bluff overlooking the confluence of the Wisconsin and Mississippi Rivers, a spot Simak returned to again and again in his fiction. He attended a one-room country school through the eighth grade and rode a horse to Patch Grove High School in the winter. His rural background crops up over and over in his settings, in his sure ear for small-town speech, and in his affectionate but accurate descriptions of natural places and things.

Simak's "Tom Sawyer" existence was leavened by a fascination with words which also began at an early age. At eight, he was already determined to learn all the words there were and how to spell them. "I had scribbled, off and on, on various subjects from the time I first started grade school...." In her introduction to Simak's bibliography, Muriel Becker wisely notes that Simak's addiction to writing is definitely not part of the image of the "All-American boy,"[3] yet Simak is in good company with Twain, Hemingway, and Fitzgerald, who also had their beginnings in the Midwest.

After a stint teaching school, Simak tried working his way through the University of Wisconsin. When the funds ran out, Simak launched his newspaper career by taking a position on the Iron River, Michigan *Reporter* and in a couple of years became editor. As a full-time newspaperman, he could afford to get married. He wed Agnes Kuchenberg (whom he refers to as Kay) in that same year, 1929. He had scratched the writing itch by becoming a journalist, but news writing did not completely satisfy his urge. He had early admired science fiction from reading Jules Verne, then graduated from Verne to Haggard and Wells, and was ready both in reading habits and inclination to welcome the magazines. To Simak, science fiction was not only a field from which he derived reading pleasure, but it was "a medium of ideas."

Although he wrote space opera and other pulp hackwork at first, he always wanted to do something different. He submitted his first short story, "The Cubes of Ganymede," to *Amazing Stories* in 1929. The story was accepted, but two years later, T. O'Conor Sloane returned the manuscript without publishing it.

Simak did sell his next story, "The World of the Red Sun," to *Wonder Stories*, and it appeared in the December, 1931 issue. In 1932, Simak sold three more stories to *Wonder* and one to *Astounding*, then suddenly left the field. Simak stopped writing science fiction except for a controversial religious fantasy, *The Creator*, printed in the semipro magazine, *Marvel Tales* (March/April 1935). He took a succession of newspaper jobs throughout the Middle West and in 1939, settled down on the staff of the *Minneapolis Star* as a copy reader. Within a year, Simak was advanced to chief of the copy desk.

Simak's new duties certainly kept him from writing science fiction during this period of his life, but part of the reason was his own dissatisfaction with what he was doing. He had his own ideas about how science fiction should be written, and in a fanzine article,[4] Simak rejected his own work written in the Gernsback mode as "mere journals of pointless adventure...mouthpieces to explain scientific apparatus and scientific theory." He wanted the science-fiction story to stand on its own two feet as a legitimate story "with characterization, human interest, humor, and deeper insight into other fundamentals of humanity and the scientific world."

This desire to write science fiction about real people may have attracted Simak to writing it again and this time for John W. Campbell, Jr., who in 1937 became editor of *Astounding*. Simak responded to Campbell's request for more believable characters with stories about football players, Iowa farmers, and old soldiers. Campbell was much taken with Simak's first novel, *The Cosmic Engineers*. Although this story was space opera in the Smith-Campbell tradition, its protagonists are middle-class citizens of the thirties, not scientists or soldiers of fortune.

From 1940 to 1942 Simak published regularly but not profusely in the magazines, mostly in *Astounding*. He suffered a writer's block and needed money, so wrote some easily forgettable aviation and cowboy stories. As Simak told it, he went out and bought a bunch of Westerns, spent the weekend reading them, and started writing to the formula. One editor billed him as "a man who knows the West so well...." Simak recalled, "Hell. I'd never been west of the Missouri River at that time."

The inspiration to write science fiction eventually returned, and Simak never again wrote any other kind of fiction. Nor did a writer's block ever again interrupt the flow of stories. In 1944, he produced eight short stories and novelettes. He wrote four of the popular Webster series in *Astounding* (which later became *City*), and sold the humorous adventures of Mr. Meek, a mousy bookkeeper transformed into a heroic rogue, to *Planet Stories*. In the late forties, his output again decreased. Simak's personal life became very busy and probably left little time to write. Son Richard Scott was born in 1947, Simak was promoted to news editor of the *Minneapolis Star* in 1949, and daughter Ellen was born in 1951. Fewer of his stories saw print, but the quality remained high. The three final Webster episodes to appear in *Astounding Science Fiction* were published in 1946 and 1947.

The fifties began another productive period and also brought Simak some well-deserved honors. In 1950 Simak had the lead in the first issue of a new magazine called *Gal-*

axy with the novel *Time Quarry*, later known as *Time and Again*. In 1952 appeared *City*, a collection of the Webster short stories from *Astounding* woven together on the framework of tales told by dogs long after man has disappeared from the face of the earth. *City* won the 1953 International Fantasy Award for fiction, and in 1958, Simak won the Hugo for his novella *The Big Front Yard*.

Simak only wrote one other novel during the fifties, *Ring Around the Sun*, but numerous short stories and novelettes poured from his pen. They have been anthologized again and again, and have established Simak's reputation as one of the best craftsmen of science fiction in the shorter form. Three hardcover collections of these tales of the fifties have been published: *Strangers in the Universe* (1956), *The Worlds of Clifford Simak* (1960), and *All the Traps of Earth and Other Stories* (1962). A later collection, *Best Science Fiction Stories of Clifford Simak* (1967), was first published in London and contains the best of this output. In addition to *Astounding*, Simak was a regular in *Galaxy*, and was also easily accepted by Tony Boucher in *The Magazine of Fantasy & Science Fiction*.

Most of these stories develop themes that have long been Simak's trademarks: his concern with technology and its effects, his nostalgia for small towns and small-town life, his compassion for aliens who are humanity's next-door neighbors, and what Thomas D. Clareson termed—the brotherhood of intelligent life in the universe. Clareson defines this xenophilia as "a vision which sees all sentient creatures...as equal parts of a single community...."[5]

In the sixties, his novels started appearing in hardcover and original paperbacks rather than first appearing in magazines. In fact, after 1961 Simak averaged just one novel per year. He won a second Hugo in 1963 for *Way Station*, and other novels—*All Flesh Is Grass*, *Time Is the Simplest Thing*, *The Goblin Reservation*—were nominated for either Hugos or Nebulas. In this period, Simak's novels were much more daring and original in concept and perhaps less "folksy," conveying a kind of mysticism and etched on a broader canvas. Also during this period, Simak turned to

18

science writing, and this new interest might have had some influence on his fiction.

In 1959, Simak left the news desk to develop a school-oriented science program, the Science Reading Series, for the *Star*'s sister newspaper, the *Minneapolis Tribune*. The program was used in more than 3,500 classrooms in the newspaper's circulation area and won several awards for Simak, including the Westinghouse Award from the American Association for the Advancement of Science (1966) and the Minnesota Academy of Science Award (1967).

In addition, Simak wrote a great deal of non-fiction, especially about current developments in science in a time of growing developments in NASA and a national preoccupation with ecology and the environment. Simak got out a weekly newspaper column and wrote four books popularizing space exploration and astronomy, evolution of intelligence, prehistoric man, and cosmology. His paleontogical interests surface in several of his later works, definitely in the novella "The Marathon Photograph" (1974) and in the novel *Mastodonia* (1978).

In 1961 Simak dabbled disastrously in the theater. Broadway beckoned in the form of a producer who approached Simak about adopting one of his very funny stories, "How-2," for the stage. The title of the play was changed to a more risqué *How to Make a Man*; it opened in Detroit and was promptly panned. Simak did not lose hope—Broadway might be kinder. The Broadway critics were less sympathetic than the Detroit critics: "A play suitable for people who only read comic books." Again, the Buck Rogers-Flash Gordon science-fiction image had overridden the genuine comedy. An embittered Simak vowed never to allow his work to be dramatized on the stage again. Despite his on-stage embarrassment, some of his short stories were scripted for radio dramas on the NBC *X Minus One* show, and a number of his stories have been under option from time to time for the movies.

Simak became feature writer for the *Minneapolis Sunday Tribune* in 1969 where he remained until his retirement in August, 1976. By the end of the sixties, Simak was rated among the top five science-fiction writers in the country. His books sold well, and he could be depended on for an original, entertaining yarn with characters that readers like, the rare quality that Algis Budrys in a *Galaxy* review found in all of Simak's successful stories.[6]

Yet Simak was not content to merely grind out unique variations of the same old themes. In the furor over the New Wave, he turned to blending fantasy elements into his science fiction, writing what Muriel Becker in the Introduction to her Simak bibliography calls the "zany" novels of the seventies, stories that belong more than ever to the "realm of faery."[7] *The Werewolf Principle* (1967) and *The Goblin Reservation* (1968) were forerunners of the change. In *Out of Their Minds* (1970), Simak is deliberately trying to be different, to break out of what David Pringle has assessed as the paradoxical reason for his appeal, his consistency.[8] Simak mingles fantasy figures with real characters, the fantasy characters actually brought to life by the power of "imagination." In an interview with Paul Walker,[9] Simak defended this breach of genre. To Simak, all imaginative stories are fantasy, and if authors limit themselves, they may "stifle the true development of the imaginative story.... It can be claimed with some logic, I suppose, that ghosts and robots do not mix, but I see no reason why they shouldn't. If a writer wants to interweave the old mythology and the new, there should be nothing to prevent it.... It was with this thought in mind that I wrote *The Goblin Reservation* and then went on to write *Out of Their Minds*." Again, the "old man" was ahead of his time, writing in a genre now officially marketed as "science-fantasy," the best-seller of the eighties.

Simak took time out to edit the *Nebula Award Stories* for 1971, the only anthology to his credit, but never slowed his steady output of fiction. In 1972 Simak wrote what he calls his personal philosophical "statement of values," the novel *A Choice of Gods*; "before," he noted, "I haven't got enough time left to restate it." With the appearance of *The Enchanted Pilgrimage* (1975), Simak began to write a purer form of fantasy set in a medieval alternate world where magic replaces science. Simak, ever conscious of his audience, also wanted to cash in on the booming market for fantasy.

20

Honors still came to the "old man" in the seventies. His ability to write prize-winning short stories had not deserted him. Three stories—the novella "The Thing in the Stone" (1971), "The Autumn Land" (1972), and "Construction Shack"(1974)—were nominated for either Hugos or Nebulas. His novel *A Heritage of Stars* (1978) received the Jupiter Award from the secondary educators. But the crowning achievement for Simak came from his peers. In 1977 he received the most prestigious honor in science fiction, the Grand Master award for lifetime achievement, at the Nebula Awards banquet where he was also the keynote speaker. Only two other writers, Robert A. Heinlein and Jack Williamson, had received this accolade to that date.

In the eighties, although Simak was well into his seventies, his powers had not seriously diminished. Some of his novels did tend to repeat earlier themes but always developed these motifs in a unique way. *Project Pope* (1981) was nominated for a Hugo, and in 1981, Simak won the Hugo and the Nebula for Best Short Story for "Grotto of the Dancing Deer." Simak was Guest of Honor for his second time at the 1981 Worldcon at Denver, and in his acceptance speech, Simak paid tribute to the unique tribe "that had given him a place around the tribal campfire."

Simak still continued to take risks at an age when, as Algis Budrys put it, a Grand Master might be "expected to retire to a porch and rock himself to sleep."[10] In 1983, Simak was forced by leukemia and emphysema into a three-year hiatus from writing. Simak's wife, Kay, had suffered arthritis for many years, and Simak had gradually assumed all the duties of running the house. Her condition worsened and she was put into a nursing home, where she died in 1985.

Simak had always said that he would have no strong reason for living after Kay was gone, but he was back in June of 1986 with a new novel, *Highway of Eternity*. In this amazingly complex novel, Simak maintained the humor, sensitivity, intelligence, and moral purpose that readers had come to expect in his fiction.

With the help of neighbors and friends, Simak continued to live and was trying to write a short story when death overtook him. On the morning of April 25, 1988, he received a blood transfusion and returned from the hospital feeling exceptionally good. In the evening, he had difficulty breathing and was taken to Riverside Medical Center in Minneapolis, where he died peacefully in his sleep.

The "old man" of science fiction would write no more. Some critics claimed to perceive despair and pessimism for the human race in Simak's writings, but his later work reflected an optimism very much at odds with his feelings at the time he wrote *City* forty years ago. With the help of other intelligent beings, Simak seemed to be prophesying another "giant step for mankind," a chance to prove that such a precious gift as life cannot all have been for nothing.

II.

THE EARLY SIMAK

Simak's first published story in the December, 1931, issue of *Wonder Stories*, "World of the Red Sun," probably did not impress too many readers with the exception of Isaac Asimov. Asimov, in his autobiography and elsewhere, has given this story more notoriety than it perhaps deserves. He was so taken with it that it was the specific story that he vividly recalls retelling to his fellow students sitting at the curb in front of the junior high school.[1]

"World of the Red Sun" is a time-travel action adventure yarn, very much crafted to the taste of *Wonder Stories* readers. The two scientist-heroes equip their airplane as a time machine. Instead of traveling a few thousand years, a glitch in their instruments sends them five million years into the future to land in the ruins of what was once Denver. They are captured by a horde of primitives who possess "the eyes of furtive beings...of hunted beasts." The travelers soon learn that all men are slaves of Golan-Kirt, a creature of pure evil, "He-Who-Came-Out-of-the-Cosmos" to rule by fear. The new arrivals must do trial by combat with Golan-Kirt, but their opponents turn out to be only figments of their own imaginations—a machine gun, marching soldiers, and a lion. Golan-Kirt himself is a fraud, an imposter, the naked brain of a 1930s' mad scientist who has ruled by fear for five million years. The intrepid time-travelers easily dispatch the madman by laughing at him. Despite the protests of the natives who want them to remain to help restore civilization, they attempt to return to the twentieth century.

And here the epilogue of this first story foreshadows some of that ironic despair for the success of the human race so dependent on its technology, which Simak would develop more concretely in *City* twenty years later. The instruments of the time travelers fail again, and they are sent farther into the future, where they find an eroded statue honoring them as saviors of the race. Like the Time Traveller in Wells's *Time Machine*, the two then realize that they are "alone at the end of the world." Such a downbeat ending was quite unusual for Gernsback fiction.

Simak wrote four more "pulpish" stories in 1932, which can easily be forgotten, three for *Wonder Stories* and one for *Astounding*. None of these stories shares the same sense of melancholy and foreboding as "World of the Red Sun," except possibly "Voice in the Void" in *Wonder Stories Quarterly* (Spring 1932). The story is standard inter-planetary adventure except for the ending. In his curiosity to solve the mysteries of the Martian religion and to wreak vengeance on the Martians for putting his buddy's brain in a cylinder, the hero discovers a terrible secret that ordinary, money-grubbing Earthmen had visited Mars a million years ago and the Martian messiah was really a terrestrial.

Surveying stories of religion in American pulp maga-zines, Sam Moskowitz calls "Voice in the Void" the first of Simak's "sacrilegious" science-fiction stories, identifying Simak as one of the first to use this "delicate topic."[2] Simak did not remember exactly why he used such a theme, but he must have had "first causes" on his mind. Between 1932 and 1938, when Simak had stopped writing science fiction for awhile, he wrote a remarkable story, "The Creator," printed in the semipro magazine, *Marvel Tales* (March/April 1935), published by William L. Crawford. The theme was so dif-ferent, questioning the existence and character of God, and its ending so disturbing that no other editor would accept it.[3]

In "The Creator" two scientist-heroes build a "time-power" machine that takes them to a super-universe where they meet a telepathic being who created Earth and the rest of the universe as a laboratory experiment. When the Crea-tor attempts to destroy the primary universe (and hence all universes), the protagonists, with the aid of other aliens who stumbled into the Creator's lair, destroy the Creator and his laboratory. The hero-narrator is not rewarded for killing "God" and saving the Universe but returns to Earth millions of years later as the tribal chief and demigod of the last inhabitants of a dying planet.

Even as early in his career as "The Creator," Simak is metaphorically exploring the nature of the universe and how it came into being. Simak himself never accepted what he called the "easy answers" of organized religion as an explanation for the purpose of life, and his efforts to search for this explanation have caused some critics to label some of his later works as "mystic." In an interview with Paul Walker, Simak declined the "honor of being a mystic writer." The mysticism that attaches to such questions as the real meaning of intelligence and the inevitability of death lies in the fact that humans do not understand these questions, but as intelligent beings, Simak believed they must try. Simak did not accept the cold, indifferent First Principle or the Deistic Great Geometer who is only concerned with the precision and orderliness of the universe, but neither could Simak accept the idea of God as a "kindly old gentleman with a long, white, flowing beard." He differed from religious believers by stating that "we cannot be so provincial as to insist that God is for man alone and for this planet alone...we have drawn our Deity on too small a scale and in doing so have done Him a grave injustice."[4]

When Simak started writing again for John W. Campbell, his stories had a much different look. The characters became more important than plot, and the dialogue, although very much of its time, moved the action and simplified the exposition. Simak's action scenes were as gripping as any other pulpster (this faculty for writing action-adventure has never deserted him), but those characteristics that have become Simak's trademark—compassion, humor, human interest, and gentle irony—distinguished a Simak story from others.

Simak's first story for Campbell was "Rule 18" (*Astounding Science Fiction*, July 1938), and though based on a silly plot, it introduces Simak's early uneasiness at the blessings of technology. In the year 2479 Mars always wins the annual Earth-Mars football game because Earth players have gone soft because of technology. A newspaper reporter (frequently a pulp hero but, being a newspaperman himself, one of Simak's favorite heroes) uncovers cheating by Earth's coach who is using a time tunnel to recruit players from Earth's past. At the end of the story, the reporter, stranded 3000 years in the past, is making his way down to Mexico to become the white Aztec god Quetzalcoatl. Simak's time travelers never seem to possess quite enough technology to get home. "Rule 18" is lightweight science fiction, yet contains that light touch of irony which draws more attention to the moral issue than a heavier or more bitter form of satire can do.

"Rule 18" did not make very much impact on the readers, except for its influence on an eighteen-year-old fan and budding writer named Isaac Asimov. Asimov, in a letter to "Brass Tacks," gave "Rule 18" a very low rating for its "incoherent" style. He received a letter from Simak asking for details so that Simak could profit from Asimov's criticism. Asimov, on a closer rereading, found nothing wrong except for Simak's technique of writing the story in separate scenes without explicit transitional passages. He wrote Simak to explain and apologize, then adopted the same device in his own stories. He also made use of what he called Simak's "cool, unadorned style," and later credited Simak with being the major influence on his style.[5]

In most of these early stories, Simak followed a standard science-fiction formula—a problem must be solved, a matter of life and death, in some interplanetary setting. His protagonists, often leaders of expeditions, seldom have any solutions. Other less "heroic" characters, cantankerous eccentrics or acknowledged failures like drunks or derelicts, snap out of their depressions or alcoholic hazes long enough to save the expedition (and occasionally the Solar System).

Frequently, the savior is an old man. David Pringle has accused Simak of dreaming of himself as an old man, that for Simak "the ultimate state of grace is to be as old as the hills."[6] In "Reunion on Ganymede" (*Astounding Science Fiction*, November 1938), Gramp Parker, old war veteran, saves Ganymede from a pack of robot monsters and captures an escaped prisoner, a dangerous murderer. In "Rim of the Deep" (*Astounding Science Fiction*, May 1940), the only Simak story ever set on the ocean bottom, old prospector

Gus saves the hero from sea-bottom pirates and, for good measure, helps the hero to squelch some Venusian aliens set on sabotaging our undersea colonies. And, in "Clerical Error" (*Astounding Science Fiction*, August 1940), an old drunk gives up his life to save an expedition stranded on Jupiter and doomed to run out of life support.

Simak's characters are "ordinary people," folksy types found in any small town in America, and his use of such characters is partly responsible for his reputation as a "pastoralist" writer. In the 1950s, he would send alien visitors to small Wisconsin towns named Millville and Willow Bend, but even in these very early stories, he introduced the small town people and their values into an interplanetary setting. Simak's second story for Campbell, "Hunger Death" (*Astounding Science Fiction*, October 1938), was the first example of this kind of story. A strange plague that starves people to death is part of a plot by Martian scientists to regain control of the Solar System. Only New Chicago on Venus, a colony of transplanted farmers from Iowa, seems relatively immune from the disease. A newspaper reporter and an alcoholic doctor stumble on the antidote, the polka-dot weed, and announce the news to the Solar System. The depressed Iowa farmers, who had been gulled into coming to Venus by an unscrupulous land company, are now rich beyond their wildest dreams. Despite a raid by a Martian spaceship, thwarted by the old town marshal at the expense of his life and the machinations of the land company, Iowa horse sense and frontier justice prevail to save New Chicago and the Solar System.

Although he seemed to accept the Wellsian stereotype of the evil Martian in these early stories, Simak was beginning to write about aliens who were friendly, cute, helpful, and certainly less menacing than the "Bug-Eyed Monsters" on the lurid magazine covers of the period. His earliest story appealing directly to the reader's sympathy for the alien is "Madness from Mars" (*Thrilling Wonder Stories*, April 1939). The Mars expedition returns with all of its astronauts dead, apparently caused by madness among the crew members. The only creature left alive on the ship is a cute little Martian fur ball. In the zoo, it drives the other animals berserk. The Martian is homesick and lonely, and in its efforts to communicate, it issues ultrasonic signals that drive Earth life insane. The hero euthanizes the poor creature whose sounds are "like the whimpers of a lost puppy on a storm-swept street"—a far cry from evil aliens bent on the destruction of mankind!

Simak tried a couple of these "evil alien" plots, but the results were always inferior. In "Shadow of Life" (*Astounding Science Fiction*, March 1943), aliens who believe in the "rightness of evil" recruit Earthmen to preach their doctrine. Eons earlier, the aliens have already scared the old, arrogant Martians into hiding in a sub-atomic universe. The humans find a weapon to fight the aliens and want the Martians to cooperate, but the Martians refuse. Only humans, the younger race and more adaptable to change, remain to take on the Evil Beings. This is one of the few stories in which the aliens are "truly" evil, but even then, Simak justifies their actions because of their creed of "no room for benevolence in the Universe." In another very mediocre story beautifully illustrated by Virgil Finlay, "The Call from Beyond" (*Super Science Stories*, May 1950), scientists working in a laboratory on Pluto to develop controlled mutations of humans let aliens in from other dimensions; they strongly resemble the scary Cobblies in *City*. The story also implies that someone in Atlantis eons ago had made the same mistake. Aliens explain the presence of supernatural beings like ghosts, goblins, incubi, imps, and other such "things that go bump in the night." Simak would develop this idea with much more humor eighteen years later in *The Goblin Reservation*.

More often than not, the *aliens* were the victims—of Terrestrial greed. In "Masquerade" (*Astounding Science Fiction*, March 1941), Earthlings, using Mercury as a base to beam solar power back to the rest of the Solar System, give little thought to the natives, the Candles who can mimic any life form, even humans. In their lust for energy, Earthmen turn them into clowns, "a troupe of mimics, absorbing alien ideas, alien ways" (p. 73). One of the Earthmen, in foiling a plot by the Mercurians to take over the power station, realizes that the Candles are not curiosities, but a victimized race of intelligent beings.

In "Tools" (*Astounding Science Fiction*, July 1942), the aliens turn the tables on the greedy Earthmen and try to effect a change in human values. A corporation, which "owns the Solar System, body and soul" by controlling its source of power, is mining Venus for radium ore (curiously, the head of the corporation is R. C. Webster, a name that Simak will use in a much different characterization in the *City* series). Simak describes a much more hostile environment on Venus than in "Hunger Death," much closer to what it actually is and not the watery jungle beloved of most writers of the period. Archie, a native Venusian, is a blob of disembodied radon gas captured in a lead jar who has learned to communicate with Earthlings. Archie, from a race without tools, has been secretly learning technology from the Earthmen. By driving one of his observers insane enough to smash his jar, Archie gets free and joins other Venusians in a group intelligence, taking over the machinery in the mining camp. The big corporation puts up a fight, which provides the action in the story, but loses its radium monopoly.

Doc, the old psychologist who understands the Venusians, gives his life to protect Archie's secret—the "purely mental" Venusians have emotions and a superior intelligence and have been experimenting with becoming "physical." Now with tools to give them physical being, they plan to build a better civilization for Earthmen. A number of themes that Simak will develop into whole novels are contained in this story: capitalistic exploitation, superior but helpful aliens, and another chance for the human race despite its moral failures. The idea that aliens can put man back on the right track became Simak's concern for the next forty years:

> Perhaps Man had gotten off on the wrong foot. Perhaps his philosophy had been all wrong even from the start. Perhaps a bit of alien philosophy, weird as it might seem at first, would be good for him (130).

In imagining wacky aliens, Simak could compete with the best. In "Hermit of Mars" (*Astounding Science Fiction*, June 1939), which seems influenced by Weinbaum's "A Martian Odyssey," bizarre flora and fauna—traveler plants, silicon eaters, and ghosts—inhabit every canal. A better story is "Ogre" (*Astounding Science Fiction*, January 1944), a very amusing adventure in which intelligent plants contrive to take over Earth by making men forget everything but listening to their music. The planet is a botanical grotesquerie: rifle trees that shoot pellets; vines that release lightning bolts; symbiotic blanket plants that can cuddle around bodies, supply food and medical attention, and even share intelligence and emotions; and the Encyclopedia, an immortal plant that can suck data from minds and from humans the knowledge of technology that intelligent plants are searching for.

Along with his fondness for aliens, Simak likes robots. They are unquestionably "human" and not in the Frankenstein or Rossum tradition—they never turn against their creators. The robots are more often used for comic relief, ancestors of C3PO and R2D2 in *Star Wars*. In "Ogre" the traders own a female robot, Nellie, a nagging cost-conscious bookkeeper robot (who speaks very ungrammatical English—would she be programmed so poorly?) who, despite being a pain in the neck, always turns up in the nick of time to save the traders' hides.

Simak's robots are more like Asimov's, faithful artifacts who desire nothing but to serve man like the loyal old retainer, Jenkins, in *City*. Simak first used the name Jenkins in "Earth for Inspiration" (*Thrilling Wonder Stories*, April 1941). A failing science-fiction writer takes the advice of his robot valet, Jenkins, and visits Old Earth for inspiration. Like the Tin Woodman of Oz, a robot Philbert has been rusting for lack of oil on an ocean bottom for ages with only his brain working. The writer finds Philbert, hooks him up to Jenkins's body, and finds in the old robot an inexhaustible supply of plots. Also in this story, Simak introduces the idea of "wild" robots who run away from their human masters and try to build their own civilization, a concept Simak later uses in the conclusion of *City*.

Another type of story from those early days that Simak never stopped writing is the time-travel story. He had a favorite time period, the time when the Earth was free of any traces of civilization and only prehistoric man and animals like the mastodon or the saber tooth tiger roamed the plains. His first expedition to this era was in "The Loot of Time" (*Thrilling Wonder Stories*, December 1938). A scientist invents a mechanical time brain (time is non-existent but a time-sense exists in the human brain), and he and two others go on a hunting expedition to the interglacial period seventy thousand years back. The scene then shifts to the fifty-sixth century, when time-travel is an everyday occurrence. Aliens are using time travel to steal and store their loot in the past, in the same era where our twentieth-century time travelers have located. After the usual battles with wild animals and an encounter with a friendly old Neanderthal, the time travelers from the past and those from the future put a stop to the Centaurians (their appearance in the past makes them responsible for the myth of the devil), but the story ends with a puzzle—why were they stealing? Perhaps Simak intended a sequel, but never got around to writing it.

In so many of the early stories like "Tools," the villains are large corporations. Greedy capitalists always seem to accompany technological advance as humanity expands its frontier in space. In "Spaceship in a Flask" (*Astounding Science Fiction*, July 1941), a humanitarian group of researchers on Mercury are seeking to find the cure for a sickness afflicting spacemen and accidentally stumble on an elixir of youth found in the sands of Mercury. The leader of the group conceals his discovery fearing that the news will not be a blessing, but will only cause economic problems, wars, and more greed.

In "Lobby" (*Astounding Science Fiction*, April 1944), cheap atomic power frightens the power companies so much that a power lobby blows up the pilot plant. The World Committee makes a deal with the criminals to let them go unpunished if they will provide the funds to complete the research. "Lobby" is an obvious appeal for international control of atomic power, rather than leaving it in the hands of private enterprise. The behavior of big business continued

to worry Simak enough that he would later make it the subject of full-length novels in the early fifties like *Ring Around
the Sun*.

Another sociological question that bothered Simak
even in these early days was his concern for humanity's future. Given humanity's unsatisfied avarice and its inclination
to use its technology to destroy whatever it touches including
itself, where will evolution lead the human race? Will some
evolutionary change make people wise up before it is too
late? Will they acquire the wisdom as well as the knowledge
to be respected members of the community of intelligent
species?

Before Simak answered these questions by displacing
humans with intelligent dogs in *City*, he wrote two transitional stories expressing these serious concerns. The first
was "Hunch" (*Astounding Science Fiction*, July 1943). The
Solar System is faced with a terrible brain drain, a disastrous
trend projected back in the twentieth century: its best minds
are losing their sanity, communications are breaking down,
and industrial and economic progress is grinding to a halt.
The only hope is Sanctuary, an asteroid sanitarium where
everyone now goes to be cured. However, returning patients
are no longer interested in their former pursuits and have
forgotten their skills and knowledge. An agent sent to Sanctuary to investigate discovers that the Asterites, the race of
the fifth planet (now the Asteroid Belt), possess the minds of
the Sanctuary patients and grant a mental peace, wiping out
"those harsher emotions that have taken man up the ladder."
The only solution to combat the creeping contagion of madness is for humans to learn to play their hunches, a new instinct to see into the future, and put those with this psi ability
in key positions.

The story presents a moral dilemma: humanity must
either continue in competition, violence, and adversity risking madness for progress or accept the Sanctuary credo of a
"better" life. Simak raises a serious doubt about the role of
evolution in the doctrine of Progress:

> If the race were doomed to madness, if evolu-
> tion had erred in bringing man along the path

he had followed, what then? If the human way of life were basically at fault, would it not be better to accept a change before it was too late? (35)

In "Sunspot Purge" (*Astounding Science Fiction*, November 1940), another story which might even be called the "pilot" for *City*, human progress is downward and all efforts seem to make no difference. The world is going nuts— suicides, murders, a wave of violence are sweeping the world. Two newspaper reporters travel five hundred years into the future and find a dead city. In old newspaper files, they read a story of declining business, increasing unemployment, a fatal economic depression, a complete slide down the scale into barbarism. The irony of it all is that sunspots, or the lack of sunspots, are the cause.

The reporters go forward, hoping that humanity will make a comeback, but after two thousand years, they find nothing. The city is gone. A heap of earthy mounds remains where mutated animals shuffle and slink, and trees and grasses have taken over.

But man is gone. He rose, and for a little he walked the Earth. But now he's swept away... Back in 1950, Man thought he was the whole works. But he wasn't so hot after all. The sunspots took him to the cleaners. Maybe it was the sunspots in the first place that enabled him to rise up on his hind legs and rule the roost. (62)

Until 1950, most of Simak's stories were bought by Campbell, but he also sold to the adventure pulp *Planet Stories*. Simak began a series of amusing stories about Mr. Meek, a mild-mannered bookkeeper who fulfills his dream of thirty years of becoming a spaceman. In the first story, "Mr. Meek—Musketeer" (*Planet Stories*, Summer 1944), Mr. Meek goes on vacation cruising the Solar System in his own spaceship. He lands on the asteroid Juno, batwings his way into a notorious miner's bar (the story is more horse opera than space opera), and wins a shoot-out over cheating in a poker game. The town wants him to be their new sheriff, but only after being threatened does Meek take the job.

Meek only wants to find the local Loch Ness monster, the Asteroid Prowler, and do some archaeological research. Meek gets his wish—he is kidnapped and dumped on the surface of Juno. Meek even acquires a sidekick, not Smiley Burnette or Gabby Hayes, but an old prospector, Stiffy Grant. The rest of the story is predictable to anyone remembering the old Saturday afternoon matinees—Meek, of course, makes friends with the terrible monster, and he and Stiffy ride the Prowler back to town. They bring the criminals to justice who are trying to steal a lost mine and in the conclusion, a meteor, loaded with radium ore, strikes Juno making Stiffy and Meek rich. The story is fun, admirably suited to *Planet*'s editorial policy, and readers liked it.

The second story, "Mr. Meek Plays Polo" (*Planet Stories*, Fall 1944), is not copied so directly from the Western formula. Mr. Meek travels to Saturn's rings, gets himself drafted as a coach in a space polo match, bets his spaceship he can win the match (one of those impulsive acts of bravado when Meek gets angered), and then must play polo himself. Aided by some of Simak's whimsical aliens (bugs with advanced math skills), Meek wins. Simak decided he had enough of Mr. Meek after two stories (he had only written them for his own amusement) and turned to more serious science fiction.

During his apprenticeship, as Simak likes to call this early period before the publication of *City*, Simak wrote only two novels, both space operas, and one not really his own, but in collaboration with John W. Campbell. Collaboration may be too strong an epithet to apply to *Empire*, a story Campbell originally wrote when he was eighteen years old. Campbell was never able to get *Empire* published—and justifiably so. When Campbell published Simak's *Cosmic Engineers* in 1939, he was quite taken with it, calling it "a power novel with sensitivity." Campbell then sent Simak *Empire* and asked him if he would rewrite it. Simak "gagged when he read it" but manfully forged ahead. His effort was somewhat better, but Campbell himself turned the rewrite down. Simak, with a sigh of relief, dutifully put *Empire* on the shelf. However, when Horace Gold was publishing *Galaxy Science Fiction Novels*, he had heard from Campbell that Simak had an unpublished story and pleaded for the right to publish it. Thus *Empire* finally saw print, but not until 1951.

Simak and Campbell were both accurate in their judgments of *Empire*—it was probably the poorest science-fiction story ever written by two men who had written some pretty good science fiction. Two super-scientists are building a spaceship with the gadgets to destroy the monopoly of a company controlling all power sources by viciously squelching all competition. The story quickly degenerates into a series of spy-counterspy moves and space dogfights with the heroes and the villains foiling each other's plots to steal their discoveries. In the Doc Smith tradition, the story ends with a spaceship showdown in interstellar space. Despite its incredible comic-book plot, some of Simak's biases are present: capitalists lusting for power, wasted resources on Earth sending men to the stars to open a new frontier, and the moral imperative of the common people to take over their own destinies.

The novel that had impressed Campbell so much was *The Cosmic Engineers*, serialized in *Astounding* (February-April 1939) and reissued in paperback in 1950. Like *Empire*, it is pure, unadulterated Smith-Campbell space opera but cleverly handled on a canvas truly cosmic. On Pluto, mysterious messages are being received from the galaxy. Two newspaper reporters, on their way to Pluto to cover the story, stumble on Caroline Adams, a scientist exiled for a thousand years of self-induced suspended animation. Caroline, a spunky female rare in pulp space opera, was declared a traitor for refusing to turn over a discovery that would have won the current war. During her long sleep, she has developed psi powers that enable her to interpret the messages. The messages are from a billion-year-old race, the Cosmic Engineers, who warn that the universe is in danger of collision with a second universe. The Engineers, in communication with the inhabitants of this second universe, have summoned the best minds from every race in the universe to solve the problem. To complicate matters further, the Engineers are at war with the Hellhounds, another evil race capable of navigating the "interspace" between universes and therefore willing to see the Universe destroyed if they can dominate the next one to form.

With the help of the Engineers, the Earthlings travel to the planet of the Engineers at the edge of the universe, where a conference of aliens (all loathsome to the humans) decides that the humans, because of their courage and imagination, must save both universes. The humans are sent millions of years into the future to get the answers from the last old man on Earth. After a number of hairbreadth escapes (once they are kidnapped by a million-year-old collective mind that has gone insane), they steal energy from the fifth dimension, destroy the Hellhounds, and save both universes.

No one can deny that this story had range and sweep—Simak showed that he could write space opera with the best. There are enough ideas left over in the novel to write several sequels, but the real interest lies in its optimistic treatment of the human race. In later novels, the brotherhood of the galaxy treats humankind as inferior, a kind of black sheep among intelligent races, in need of education into proper use of its abilities. But in *The Cosmic Engineers*, humans have been selected to save the universe because of their imagination and vision, qualities the mechanistic Engineers, a race of robots created three billion years ago by a race from whom humanity has descended, have never evolved over all these eons. Yet Simak remained uneasy about humanity's readiness to take too many giant steps forward. When the Engineers offer the Earthlings their marvelous city, the humans turn the Engineers down:

> ...We'd just make a mess of things. We'd have too much power, too much leisure, too many possessions. It would smash our civilization and leave us one in its stead that we could not manage. We haven't put our own civilization upon a basis that could coincide with what is here.
>
> ...Sometime in the future. When we have wiped out some of the primal passions. When

we have solved the great social and economic
problems that plague us now. When we have
learned to observe the Golden Rule...when we
have lost some of the lustiness of youth.
Sometime we will be ready for this city
(Chapter 18).

In reading Simak's "apprentice" stories, pulpish and
badly written as they may seem compared to Simak's more
mature work beginning with the *City* stories, the seeds of
ideas are found that will sprout and grow over and over in
many later stories. All his major themes that he will use
again and again are contained in embryo in these early stories: the criticism of human society for its failure to use the
gifts of technology for its own improvement, the greed of
large corporations who use technology to expand their cor-
porate empires into the Solar System and to the stars, the
community of intelligent races who sit in judgment on human actions, and the prospects of the evolution of the human
race into a worthy member of this galactic brotherhood.

Also, in these early stories, Simak was gently but
firmly taking on the responsibility of being the moral conscience of the human race. It was never Simak's way to be a
polemicist—he told Thomas D. Clareson that "anger is useless," and that "he always remained pretty good-
natured...attitudes baldly expressed have no place in fiction...." But in the "City" stories, which came shortly after
this early period, Simak found an expression for his doubts
about the human race and where it was going.

III.

CITY

Certainly no other work of Simak's has ever been more of a favorite than *City*. *City* has never been completely out of print since it was first published in 1952, except for a brief hiatus in the very late '80s and early '90s. In fact, its overwhelming success sometimes perturbed Simak, "because I haven't written anything as popular since." The novel established Simak as a major writer and brought him to the attention of the world, especially to British fandom. *City* won the International Fantasy Award (IFA) in 1953, ranking Simak with such prestigious company as Arthur C. Clarke and J. R. R. Tolkien. (The Hugos finally did the IFA in, but before the Hugos were established, the IFA was the gold medal of the science-fiction Olympics.)

No single work of Simak's, with the possible exception of *Way Station*, reflects the theme of the human race's unworthiness to be the dominant species any more clearly than *City*. Thomas D. Clareson, in one of the first full-length studies of Simak's work, goes so far as to say that no one but Simak in *City* had so thoroughly "condemned man's surrender to that technology which had led him to Hiroshima and the Moon—not even those who howled in guilt in the years immediately following World War Two or those who pictured dystopia as early as the 1950's."[1]

In the author's foreword to the 1976 Ace reprint of *City*, Simak confessed to his own moral and intellectual despair at the carnage of World War II, especially the bombing of Hiroshima, and to his disillusionment with the belief that technology was the key to inevitable progress. (This puts Simak's sociological conscience twenty years ahead of the alienated group of New Wave writers, but then he was always ahead of the pack providing inspiration to younger writers.) The combination of human cussedness with its success at technology led Simak to visualize doomsday:

There is nothing wrong with technology as such; what is wrong is our preoccupation with it. We have made a god out of our machines; in many ways we have sold our souls to them (2).

Such arch-conservatism makes one wonder how Simak ever got himself published by John W. Campbell, but apparently this anti-technological attitude never bothered Campbell, for seven of the eight tales which later became *City* were published in *Astounding* between 1944 and 1947.

The novel *City* is actually a collection of framed tales, most of which were published in *Astounding* as separate short stories. The eight tales are "City" (1944), "Huddling Place" (1944), "Census" (1944), "Desertion" (1944), "Paradise" (1946), "Hobbies" (1946), "Aesop" (1947), and "The Trouble with Ants" (1951). The first seven appeared in *Astounding*, but Simak was forced to sell the final tale to *Fantastic Adventures*. Campbell did not like the idea of ants inheriting the earth.

Simak tacked these eight tales on the framework of a legend that Dogs tell "when the fires burn high and the wind is from the north." The story begins in a future when the world has literally gone to the dogs and "Man" has become a myth. The Dogs dispute among themselves about the existence of such concepts as cities, wars, and mankind itself. Could there have been such a perverse creature as Man? Was it possible that, in some primeval time, Man and Dogs were actually friends? In the "Editor's Preface," the Dog reader is cautioned against taking "these tales too much to heart, for complete confusion, if not madness, lies along this road."

On this heavily ironic note, Simak begins his future human history. To add to the fun of the story, each of the tales is preceded by a head note providing satirical, scholarly comments by the Dogs. The arguments are delightfully tongue-in-cheek. Here is how the Dogs feel about accepting the idea of a city: most Dog authorities "regard such an organization as a city as an impossible structure, not only from the economic standpoint, but from the sociological and physiological as well." The Dogs cannot believe that any creature with the nervous system to develop a culture "could survive within such restricted limits. The result...would lead to mass neuroticism which in a short time would destroy the very culture which built the city."

Simak was personally never able to abide a city. Although he worked in Minneapolis for more than thirty years, he fled to suburbia as soon as he could. In the 1976 Foreword to *City*, he warned:

> I believed then, and I believe even more strongly now, that the city is an anachronism we'd be better off without...Today's typical city is a glittering downtown business section surrounded by growing rings of ghettos. At one time...there was reason for the city. Men first huddled in it for safety, later stayed huddled in it to conduct their business. The city no longer is a defensive structure; in fact, in most cases, it is safer outside the city than in it (3).

The first tale, "City," begins in 1992. Industry has been decentralized by the threat of atomic war. With the promise of cheap land and the convenience of the family airplane, the people have deserted the cities and fled to the country except for some "squatters" and diehards like John Webster. Webster too very much wants to leave but has remained in the city out of a deep sense of duty. After a final eloquent plea trying to convince the City Council that the cities are indeed dead, Webster resigns as President of the Chamber of Commerce, planning to minister to the technologically unemployed. But when the squatters threaten civil war if the Council burns the houses, Webster tries unsuccessfully to stop the Council. Before any serious bloodshed, the crisis is resolved by one of those ironic twists of fate that

When the Fires Burn High and the Wind Is from the North

Simak sprinkled all through the novel. Adams, a former urban resident, has bought the city for back taxes, planning on turning it into a memorial museum.

The second tale, "Huddling Place," is set in the year 2117 A.D., six generations of Websters later. The Websters have lived on the land for two-hundred years and never go anywhere. Their personal needs are attended to by robots like the faithful retainer, Jenkins. As a consequence of this flight from the cities, "the huddling places," Jerome Webster is afflicted with agoraphobia. Another crisis faces the Websters—Jerome is asked to come to Mars, where he had formerly spent five years studying the physiology of the Martian brain, to save the life of his old Martian friend, Juwain the philosopher. Juwain has developed a concept that will advance mankind ten thousand years in the space of two generations. After an agonizing internal struggle, Webster screws up his courage...but too late; faithful Jenkins has sent the rescue ship away.

In the third tale, "Census," Simak introduces the talking dogs. Sixty-six years after Jerome Webster's failure, Richard Grant, a government agent taking the first census in three-hundred years, meets Nathaniel, a talking dog, while he is prowling the Webster estates.[2] To palliate the guilt felt by the Websters over the loss of Juwain, Bruce Webster, Jerome's grandson, has been experimenting with dogs, granting the dogs the gift of speech in the hope that two intelligent but dissimilar races working together might improve the human condition. Jerome's son, Grandfather Thomas, is still alive at eighty-six. He designed the first starship, now on its way to Alpha Centauri with his son Allen aboard. Thomas had help from the mysterious, long-lived mutants, descendants of squatters and farmers, who are hiding out in the hills.

Grant is also searching for the mutants in the hope that they might be able to interpret Juwain's remaining notes—his real mission, not the census. After leaving the Websters, Grant encounters the mutant Joe, who helped Thomas Webster build the starship. With a growing apprehension for the future of humankind, Grant realizes that the mutants have no need of human approval and certainly no

41

desire to preserve the human race. For his own amusement, Joe has hastened the evolution of a colony of ants by enclosing their anthill with a glass dome. (The ants have already learned how to smelt ore.) Joe looks at Juwain's papers, but refuses to share his insights with Grant. When Grant threatens him, Joe knocks Grant out and steals the Juwain notes. In the final scene of the story, Grant charges the dogs to carry on the dream of progress.

In these first three tales, Simak shows how humanity is slowly but steadily losing its grip on its own destiny. Technology has improved—robots that are almost human, interstellar travel, genetic transformation of species—yet humans cannot reverse their downward trend. The next evolutionary step is the mutants, but they reject any human interests, even trying a genetic experiment of their own to undermine the dominance of Homo sapiens. The Websters might have given humanity a second chance, but they fumbled it. Aware of the coming disaster, the Websters have taken some steps to prevent it with the talking dogs, but indecision has made them powerless.

Jerome Webster's agoraphobia is a symptom of the

> growing unwillingness of men...following the breakup of the cities to move from familiar places, a deepening instinct to stay among the scenes and possessions which in their mind have become associated with the contentment and graciousness of life.

This tendency towards solitary pleasures and withdrawal from the affairs of humankind has now been bred into humans' evolutionary successors, the mutants. The mutants completely lack any altruistic feelings and will do nothing to help the race from which they sprang. In fact, the mutants seem to be actively planning the destruction of humanity. Joe's experiment with the ants could lead to the insects' eventual takeover if not restrained by the dogs.

In the fourth tale, "Desertion," the stage is set for the disappearance of the human race from the Earth. The scenario is moved off Earth to Jupiter. Attempts to colonize

Jupiter have failed consistently. To withstand the dangerous climate, explorers have been changed by a matter converter into Lopers, the indigenous Jovian life-form. Kent Fowler, head of Dome No. 3, Jovian Survey Commission, has sent five men into the howling maelstrom of the giant planet, but none have returned. To solve the mystery, Fowler, accompanied by his aging dog, Towser, decides to find out for himself.

On the surface of Jupiter, Fowler and Towser discover a whole new world of sensations, a whole new sense of being. Their intelligence has been augmented, and they can now communicate telepathically. The mystery of the missing men has been solved—they have deserted the human race for the good life of a Loper. Fowler and his dog cannot resist the temptation to stay, either.

"They would turn me back into a dog," said Towser.
"And me," said Fowler, "back into a man."

In the fifth tale, "Paradise," Fowler has forsaken the paradise of Jupiter to do his duty and returned to human form, leaving Towser on Jupiter. Fowler is faced with a difficult decision. Should people be told about this Jovian Eden and risk a mass exodus from Earth? Tyler Webster, Chairman of the World Committee, opposes making the knowledge of Jupiter public, fearing the end of the human race. Fowler, however, angry at the blunders of the Websters and calling them a jinx on humanity, threatens to tell the world.

Things had been looking up for the human race before Fowler returned with his dangerous secret. There have been a thousand years of peace on the Earth, no murders have been committed for 125 years, and with the help of the dogs, the telepathic mutants have been carefully watched. Webster receives a call from Joe (still alive!), who now offers humans the Juwain philosophy. Without revealing to Webster what the mutants want, Joe explains that Juwain's philosophy provides an empathic-telepathic, quasi-mystical capability to sense the viewpoint of another person. "With

43

ROBERT J. EWALD

Juwain's philosophy you have to accept the validity of another man's ideas and knowledge, not just the words he says, but the thought back of the words." One of the few faults in *City* is this Juwain philosophy, a sentimental ambiguity that contrasts so sharply with the ironic tone of the rest of the story.

After Joe's call, Webster looks through a kaleidoscope he bought for his child and feels a sudden wrench. When Fowler returns to talk, Webster pleads for time, but surprisingly now, he understands Fowler's point of view—he has acquired the Juwain philosophy. Over the city, the mutants have placed a neon sign with flashing colors, the counterpart of the kaleidoscope that gave Webster the Juwain conversion. Now the whole human race has been converted, and Webster perceives the mutants' master plan to end human civilization. With the Juwain philosophy and the news about Jupiter, humankind will most certainly desert the planet. The mutants will be free to develop any kind of society they wish.

As at the beginning of the tale when Fowler was faced with the decision to reveal the Jovian paradise, Webster also must decide whether or not to kill Fowler. But Webster cannot do it—a millennium without violence has made settling an issue by killing impossible.

In these last two tales, the flight of humanity to Jupiter perpetuates the flight from the cities and is another step down in humanity's diminishing dominance as a species. Humankind has completely forsaken its formerly strong sense of destiny, its drive for progress, and has literally escaped into another plane of existence. Those who have labeled Simak a pastoral writer may be seeing pastoralism with a vengeance. The generally accepted view of pastoralism is that pastoralists encourage urban dwellers to abandon the cities for a more "natural" existence in an Edenic countryside where all anyone has to do all day is tend the sheep, dance around the Maypole, and live like Adam and Eve before the temptation. The conversion of humankind into an alien race seems a bitterly ironic reward for such human aspirations. Such irony may have led some critics like Jason Pascoe to label Simak "in general black and pessimistic."[3]

44

However, for humanity, there are blacker days to come. At the beginning of the sixth tale, "Hobbies," a thousand years have passed. Most of the human race has departed for Jupiter, except for a little colony of five thousand still living in Geneva. All of the old respected institutions have vanished with the humans: government, law, commerce, religion, and even the family. Under the influence of Juwainism, people have lost their sense of purpose, their desire for achievement, and are busy following hobbies instead of work. Jon Webster leads such a useless life, writing the history of Geneva in despair for the human condition. His former wife, Sara, announces her intention to pursue an alternative to this boring, senseless paradise by taking the Sleep, a state of suspended animation, hoping to awake sometime in a better future. Webster's son, Tom, has returned to the woods and lives off the land.

Webster pays a visit to his ancestral home where the dogs and Jenkins, now two thousand years old, are delighted to serve a Webster again. Jenkins brings Webster up to date. The dogs have developed psychic powers and are listening for Cobblies, fearful creatures from another dimension. (One of the dogs, Ebenezer, cures Webster's warts.) Wild robots are building machines for some unknown purpose, and the mutants are holed up in their castles. Jenkins confesses that dogs and robots need human leadership once again to build a civilization based on the brotherhood of animals.

Webster, however, no longer considers his species worthy to lead the dogs on their new path, "it must not be tainted by the stale breath of man's thinking." Before he goes into the Sleep himself for eternity, Webster activates the mechanism isolating the remnant of the human race in Geneva, giving the dogs their chance.

"Aesop," the seventh tale, leaps ahead another five thousand years. Jenkins is celebrating his 7000th birthday, and the dogs have given him the present of a new body. Technology has been left to the wild robots. The animals, with their robot companions, have built a civilized society under the guidance of the dogs. Killing is absolutely forbidden, causing a bad problem of over-population. The wild

45

robots are building starships, and the dogs have probed into time travel in an effort to siphon off the growing numbers. A remnant of humanity exists, known under the generic term of "websters," the descendants of Jon's son and some others caught outside when Geneva was cut off.

Jenkins tries to keep the memories of humanity's achievements and the glory of the Websters alive. However, the old human way of thought is threatening to come back. One of the websters, Peter, has killed a robin with his bow and arrow. Jenkins must solve the "bow-and-arrow" problem before killing spreads again. He seeks out the mutants for help, but finds they have departed for other worlds.

The dogs are seeking ways to travel to the alternate worlds of the Cobblies to relieve the population pressure. The murderer Peter and the wolf Lupus meet one of the Cobblies. When the Cobbly kills Lupus, Peter's psychic projection of hate frightens the Cobbly back to his own world. Jenkins arrives on the scene in time to read the incantation from the Cobbly's frantic mind. Jenkins now knows what he must do. At the webster picnic, Jenkins recites the incantation, transporting himself and the whole human race into the Cobbly world, finally eradicating the human species from Earth.

The old robot, Jenkins, is the only one left with the knowledge of human values, and he has kept the myth of humanity alive only out of an ingrained sense of duty to his former masters, the Websters. Only when he at last accepts the fact that human nature will never change, does he realize that the dogs have built a better society without technology, and have developed other powers always latent in intelligent beings. In later stories, Simak postulated other human civilizations founded on some other basis besides technology, and psi powers were often among these possible alternatives.

"Hobbies" poses the issue candidly—is humanity worth saving? And obviously, it is not. Only a remnant of humankind remains, most human institutions are abolished, and those humans left are parasites living in Geneva off the capital of their ancestors (Simak's selection of Geneva is curious, probably because it has always been the center of international peace negotiations?) and leading a boring, useless existence. Many of those remaining have already chosen a form of death-in-life, suspended animation, as much of an agent of desertion as their ancestors becoming Jovian Lopers. Jon Webster could be performing the last heroic human act by giving the dogs their chance, or perhaps he is only ending the ennui of his own worthless life and the rest of humanity.

"Aesop" finishes the human race off by sending it to an alternate universe, where, given humanity's predisposition, it could become a "boogie man" to the Cobblies. Peter Webster's rediscovery of the human instinct for killing other species completes the old robot's disillusionment and gives Jenkins an excuse to get rid of the whole cussed species, leaving the world to the nobility of the dogs. Such an ironic and appropriate ending for the human race is imagined by Simak without the bitterness of a Swift or the bleakness of an Orwell.

The eighth and final tale of *City*, "The Simple Way," is set ten thousand years later after "Hobbies" (about 13,500 A.D.). The peace of the Brotherhood of Beasts is threatened by Joe's experiment with the ants. The dogs have discovered how to travel to alternate worlds and have set up a lottery to relieve the population pressure. Homer, the leader of the dogs, visits the wild robots and hears from Andrew, a 10,000-year-old robot, the story of man and the dogs and the tale of the mutant Joe and the ants. One day Joe broke the glassite dome that covered the ants and scattered the ants with his foot. The liberated ants have erected a mighty building covering the area of a township and are obviously planning on taking over the Earth. To get help, the ants plant tiny devices resembling fleas on the animals that irresistibly summon the animals' robots to work on the building.

Jenkins returns from the alternate world to help Homer (the humans disappeared four thousand years ago). Should the dogs desert to the Cobbly worlds and leave the Earth to the ants? Jenkins goes to Geneva to seek advice from the last remaining websters. He awakens Jon Webster, but Webster's solution is typically human—poison the ants. But the dogs have no chemistry—and no art of killing for five thousand years, not even a flea.

47

Once more Jenkins has foolishly asked humankind for advice and the answer is—"Exterminate the brutes!" The human race knows only one solution—kill the other fellow if he stands in your way. The superior species of the Dogs, who believe in brotherhood and despise hatred and killing, have learned to solve their problems of overpopulation and competition from the ants by the simple non-violent expedient of moving away, also surrendering one of humanity's most cherished and fought-for values, property rights.

In a final "City" story, fittingly entitled "Epilog," written thirty years later for a John W. Campbell Memorial Anthology edited by Harry Harrison, Simak returns to the Earth and the faithful robot, Jenkins, who has now become almost human. When the Dogs left for the Cobbly worlds, Jenkins remained at Webster House with its memories. The ants enclosed the world with their building, but left Webster Hill and its adjoining five acres untouched. Jenkins spies a crack in the ants' building. He investigates and finds the ants have all gone. Nothing is left inside the ant's colossal edifice but monstrous ant hills, and on top of each ant hill a strange ornamental cast in the form of a kicking foot.

The Earth is lonely and without living things except for Jenkins and some meadow mice. As Jenkins is speculating on the fate of the ants, a starship lands. The old robot, Andrew, steps out. Andrews invites Jenkins to go with him to the stars where he can be of service again. Sadly, Jenkins leaves, but he cannot forget nor can he say goodbye..."If he could only weep, he thought, but a robot cannot weep."

Like most of Simak's serious work, *City* is saved from the label of "doomsday" literature by its lighter touch. All turns out right in the end. The human race does not really destroy itself, nor does Simak permit the loss of intelligent life on Earth. Humanity is merely shuffled off to a new world, a new frontier where perhaps human ambition and the inevitable human cussedness could begin all over again.

From the time Simak wrote the original stories in the forties and the first publication of *City*, he had time to reflect upon his reasons for writing *City*. He later saw *City* as a fictional "counterbalance to the brutality through which the world was passing," a response to the fear and anxiety generated by the hydrogen bomb and an expression, in Simak's gentle way, of his disgust for humanity's misuse of its gifts.

But there were other ways of nudging the human conscience, and what better way than by interference from outside? The national UFO craze to see aliens in every meteor shower and the bad treatment of aliens by the monster movies excited Simak's compassion for a new underdog, the alien visitor. Who would be better suited to get humankind back on the track than our unseen neighbors, the aliens among us?

IV.

STRANGERS IN THE UNIVERSE

In one of the two long major critical overviews of Simak's work published in the late seventies,[1] Thomas D. Clareson highlighted a major theme in Simak's work in the fifties and early sixties, a theme that Simak never ceased using, shaping, and developing in his fiction. Clareson called this theme the brotherhood of intelligent life:

...Simak attempts to enunciate a vision which sees all sentient creatures, however diverse their forms, as equal parts of a single community which is itself the purpose and meaning of the galaxy.[2]

To Simak, intelligence is the *summum bonum* in the universe, and all sentient beings have a moral imperative to respect the gift of intelligence. When humanity misuses its intelligence for power or profit, as it does all too often in Simak's fiction, other intelligent life forms come forward to correct the abuses. To save the human species from itself and the self-destructive fruits of its technological progress, aliens take on the burden of making humans more acceptable members of this advanced community by educating them or speeding up their evolutionary processes. Simak also accepted the premise that human beings contain latent psi powers that only need the right alien stimulation to develop.

Aliens saving the universe from humanity is certainly an ironic reversal of the customary role of the alien in science fiction. In the history of science fiction, whether aliens arrive in spaceships or slither through from other dimensions, they traditionally have been enemies of the human race. H. G. Wells's Martians set the mark of Cain on all sub-sequent visitors from other worlds and established their reputation as invaders bent on genocide, or at the very least, enslavement. Pulp magazine science fiction with its lurid covers featuring menacing BEMs (bug-eyed monsters) fixed the horrible alien into a cliché. And with the spate of alien invasion movies in the 1950s, Hollywood further cemented the image of the frightening alien in the popular imagination and, to some extent, in the psyche of the hardened science-fiction fan. After a rash of sightings in the late 1940s, alien invaders in flying saucers soon became a part of the iconography of science-fiction art in the fifties. Many writers played upon UFO fears of alien invasions and Communist conspiracies—good examples of this kind of paranoia were Heinlein's *Puppet Masters* (1951) and Jack Finney's *Invasion of the Body Snatchers* (1955), especially the B film classic made from Finney's novel the very same year.

Simak, with his customary compassion for anything downtrodden, thought that aliens were getting a raw deal from both his fellow science-fiction writers and the media. They had been cast in the role of heavies too long. Despite their green skin and tentacles, aliens could be "just folks" like anybody else in the universe, friends and neighbors from the far reaches of the galaxy. They might not always come to eat us, kill us off, or turn us into slave labor—they could come to help us.

And, occasionally, we could help them. Brian W. Aldiss remarks in *Billion Year Spree* that Simak's aliens are generally "men without sin," creatures possessing virtues that humans have lost in their Faustian preoccupation with technology. Aldiss described Simak's sympathetic extra-terrestrial encounters with this tongue-in-cheek plot analysis:

> There was a time when Simak was every-one's favorite author. A Simak story was un-mistakable. When everyone else appeared to be describing big tough heroes going out and giving alien races what-for, Simak would tell you about this little old Earthman sitting on his verandah, whittling a stick when up comes

this green guy. The green guy has a funny big machine come down out of the skies. The two of them get to talking, and the little old Earthman takes a can of oil and fixes the green man's funny big machine, and in exchange this green guy makes the little old Earthman's crops grow a durn sight better'n his neighbour's ever do.[3]

1. THE ALIEN SHORT STORIES

Certainly Aldiss has oversimplified and stereotyped Simak's aliens, but he has captured the spirit in which Simak approached this type of story in the fifties. The motif of alien visitors almost completely dominated the major part of Simak's work in this period. Of the sixty-three short stories published from 1950 to 1965, forty-seven featured aliens or robots and one sentient space ship. Of the eight novels published during this same period, six dealt with alien visitors or alien influence.

Although Simak continued to sell to Campbell, a new magazine, *Galaxy*, edited by Horace L. Gold, received the best of these alien stories. In fact, the inaugural issue of *Galaxy* (October 1950) featured the first installment of one of Simak's rare novels in this period, *Time Quarry*, later released in book form as *Time and Again*. Of the forty-seven "alien" short stories, *Galaxy* and its companion, *Worlds of If*, published twenty-two, nearly half. *Astounding* printed only six, *The Magazine of Fantasy & Science Fiction* four, and *Amazing Stories* three, while the others were scattered among the plentiful but short-lived magazines of the fifties.

Because of his enormous output of short stories in the 1950s and early 1960s, some critics and fans think of Simak as primarily a short story writer, and for nine years after the success of *City* in 1952, he wrote only one novel, *Ring Around the Sun*. Simak devoted himself to writing short stories, turning out only an occasional longer story that never exceeded novella length.[4] Many of these excellent stories were collected in three major anthologies: *Strangers in the*

Universe (1956), *The Worlds of Clifford Simak* (1960), and *All the Traps of Earth and Other Stories* (1962).

Simak divided his stories about equally between visits of aliens to Earth, and Earthling's encounters with aliens on off-world expeditions. When the aliens come to Earth, they arrive quietly, bearing a variety of miraculous gifts: immortality, the elixir of youth, immunity from disease, or a quality sadly lacking among most humans—a sense of compassion and concern for others. The neighbor in "Neighbor" (*Astounding Science Fiction*, June 1954) is an alien who has transformed Coon Valley into a paradise: no sickness, no danger, no disaster, and no crop failure. Those who try to leave—and who wants to leave?—cannot seem to find the main road. The perfect babysitters of "The Sitters" (*Galaxy*, April 1958) are benign aliens who transfer the gift of youth to the older citizens of Millville by literally stealing it from the young.

Aliens are the source of what humans choose to call good or bad luck. In "Galactic Chest" (*Original Science Fiction Stories*, September 1956), a reporter, investigating an "epidemic" of good luck stories, finds the cause to be alien Brownies performing acts of love and kindness, neighborliness, and brotherhood. (When the Brownies tried to contact us in the past, they became the subjects of folk tales and superstitions.) And in a variant of the same theme, "No Life of Their Own" (*Galaxy*, August 1959), Cobbly-like creatures from another dimension, who can take on the appearance of whomever they adopt, are the good or bad fairies of legend responsible for human successes or failures. To add to its charm, this story is told from a child's point of view. Alien children play with human children without a hint of racial prejudice.

In a poignant story bordering on sentimentality, two stranded aliens bring love and compassion into a little boy's cruel world in "Contraption" (*Star Science Fiction Stories, No. 1* [1953]). Mistreated by harsh foster parents, a lonely orphan boy finds a "contraption" in a blackberry patch that "feels" friendly.   The aliens, trapped and dying in their spaceship, give Johnny a jewel in exchange for his knife. When the boy returns home that night expecting a beating for being late, the jewel falls out of his pocket, and Uncle Eb and Aunt Em become downright friendly and lovable.

Sometimes the gifts achieve unexpected results and radically change the course of human behavior, the story ending with an ironic jab at Simak's favorite targets, technology and capitalism. In "So Bright the Vision" (*Fantastic Universe*, August 1956), Earth has a monopoly on writing imaginative literature because of its "yarners," writing machines that supply plots and characters. (If one reads computer-written poetry, "yarners" are no longer future technology.) An alien "blanket" brings the gift of writing without a machine to a writer down on his luck. The writer finds the alien crying in an alley and takes it in. Another alien, a biologist, invented the "blanket" from a science-fiction story (here Simak is referring to his own 1944 story "Ogre") and offers the writer money for his alien friend. Without the comfort of his "blanket," the writer has rediscovered the lost art of writing and decides to travel around the galaxy writing about his experiences.

A similar strange gift is received by an old recluse stamp collector in "Leg. Forst." (*Infinity*, April 1958). The old man receives an alien "stamp" that turns into a yellow "goop," an alien intelligence with a passion for orderliness and a zest for work. The goop cleans up the old man's junkyard apartment, then turns his attention to the rest of Earth. As the spores spread, the whole Earth, including the business community, is on its way to becoming honest and orderly.

Probably the most representative of these benevolent alien stories is "Shotgun Cure" (*The Magazine of Fantasy & Science Fiction*, January 1961). An alien offers humanity a vaccine that will cure all ills for life—free of charge with no strings attached. He makes the offer to a poor small town doctor in Millville. The alien has difficulty in understanding the economics of the human medical profession. Doc Kelly defends the system: "We are doing all we can to destroy our jobs." But the alien counters, "This is fine...It is what I thought, but it did not square with your planet's business sense" (40).

Before he believes in the alien cure, Doc asks why the aliens are being so generous. The alien replies:

"In a million years you'll know...you'll do the same yourself, but it will be something different...do not think of us as benefactors nor as supermen... Think of me...as the man across the street" (41, 43)

On the eve of "Operation Kelly," when world-wide clinics will administer the vaccine to all humankind, Doc has second thoughts. Millville had been the pilot project, and the doctor discovers that he, like others in the town, is losing some of his mental sharpness. He cannot but wonder: has intelligence also been a "disease"? Would the aliens so limit humanity's powers of self-destruction even if it meant reducing him to abject stupidity? He is willing to take the chance: "Doc had been a doctor too long to stop Operation Kelly" (48). Besides the theme of universal brotherhood, Simak rides two other favorite hobbyhorses in this slight story, the distrust of technological progress and the questionable morality of the business ethic.

Alien visitors are not always treated with hospitality, for humans, in their greed to make a buck, try to exploit the aliens. In "The Money Tree" (*Venture Science Fiction*, July 1958), aliens with the power to control plants are gulled into growing money on trees, but when they realize that they have been used as instruments for one man's greed, they uproot their trees and leave.

More often than not, the aliens are not so gullible. Human exploitation schemes backfire with sudden but funny results. In "Carbon Copy" (*Galaxy*, December 1957), a greedy realtor is approached by a Mr. Steen (he must be an alien—he is wearing his shoes on the wrong feet), making him an offer no real estate agent can refuse. For a ten percent fee, Homer can lease the same fifty houses over and over again when his clients mysteriously move away, leaving their houses empty. Homer investigates and finds that his clients have moved into dimensional extensions or "carbon copies" of the first house. Homer is rapidly becoming a wealthy man until another alien shows up. The second alien informs Homer that the housing project will be destroyed and that Mr. Steen is an alien practical joker who came to

Earth with the wrong plan—something else is in store for us. The aliens commit ritual suicide and leave Homer holding the bag, the victim of a final prank—the bags are full of worthless $20,000 bills.

"Crying Jag" (*Galaxy*, February 1960) is the outrageous story of Wilbur, an alien who gets drunk on sorrow. The janitor at the local sanitarium decides that Wilbur would make the perfect confessor and cons the local psychiatrist into paying $7000 for Wilbur's services. Another alien, Jake, warns that Wilbur is a renegade on his home planet, but the janitor ignores Jake's warning, telling Jake that he will take all the aliens he can supply. The next morning the Earth is overrun with alien confessors—everyone on Earth can have an alien of his own.

Very frequently, the alien visitor is attracted to humans who are friendless—the outcasts, the village pariahs. In "Idiot's Crusade" (*Galaxy*, October 1954), an alien visitor, convinced that *Homo sapiens* is a "treacherous and unprincipled species" inhabits the body of the village idiot, increasing his psi powers. The idiot uses his gift to reform the town and to revenge himself with ruthless justice on those who had made his life miserable. Then, he decides to extend his "crusade" to the whole world. Simak was usually not that tough on the whole human race; only one "ugly human" at a time deserved to get taken by the alien.

In the best of these alien visitor stories, the alien is stranded on Earth, a stranger in a strange land. He encounters human compassion from so-called "second-class" citizens who are not appalled at the alien's strangeness and make no attempt to use him for their own ends. In one of Simak's funnier tales, "Operation Stinky" (*Galaxy*, April 1957), a skunk-like alien takes a shine to an old drunken bum Asa, who lives near an Air Force base. The alien turns Asa's old car into a flying machine, naturally arousing the attention of the local flyboys. The military promptly seizes the alien in the name of national security to employ his superior talents on a spaceship project. Stinky helps them build the spaceship, then takes off for home, leaving the Air Force with egg on its face.

The very best of these "E.T." stories is one of Simak's
most frequently anthologized stories, "A Death in the House"
(*Galaxy*, October 1959). An alien vegetable crashes his
spaceship on the property of an old hermit farmer, Mose.⁵
Mose tries to find help in his community for the injured
alien, but everyone naturally turns him away. Not realizing
his dying alien is a plant, Mose buries the alien in his garden.
The alien, of course, comes up again in the spring. He per-
suades Mose to help him rebuild his wrecked spacecraft, and
in exchange for Mose's tenderness and "humanity," the alien
leaves Mose his most precious gift, his only companion on
the long, lonely interstellar journey home. This tender and
moving story rises above sentiment to demonstrate the power
of love among brothers of any species.

In this fifteen-year period, Simak only wrote three
"nasty" alien short stories in which the visitors actually come
to Earth in the present with malicious intentions: "Skirmish"
(*Amazing*, December 1950), originally entitled "Bathe Your
Bearings in Blood"; "Goodnight Mr. James" (*Galaxy*, March
1951), originally entitled "The Night of the Puudly"; and
"The Golden Bugs" (*The Magazine of Fantasy & Science
Fiction*, June 1960).⁶ "Skirmish" is such an untypical anti-
technology story, concerning an invasion of aliens who ani-
mate a revolt of the machines against their human masters,
that one wonders why it was reprinted and anthologized so
often. It ends with the newspaperman hero taking a stand to
fight against the machines and his defiance only a "skirmish"
in humanity's battle for freedom.

"Goodnight Mr. James" is Simak's best in this genre,
the chilling account of Henderson James, an alien psychologist suffering from temporary amnesia. When his memory
returns, he remembers he must seek out and kill a *puudly*, a
dangerous alien whose instincts for self-preservation make it
hate all living things. A *puudly* is difficult to kill because it
can implant thoughts into its victim's minds. The situation is
even more urgent because the *puudly* is about to bud. James
is able to kill the alien, but with its dying thought, the *puudly*
calls James a "half-thing, a duplicate." James realizes that if
he goes home, he will be killed because "duplicates" are not
allowed to live after they have served their purpose. James

has two choices if he wants to remain alive—either confront the original Mr. James and make a deal or flee. He chooses to see James, sneaks into his house, but finds it empty. The duplicate James orders the execution of the original (and here it is almost a shame to give away this O. Henry ending in this plot summary). Suddenly the telephone rings—it is the duplication lab. They did this duplicate differently—"an experiment, slow poison in the bloodstream...twenty-four hours...like a time bomb."

"It was good of you to let me know," said James.
"Glad to," said Allen. "Good night, Mr. James."

"Goodnight Mr. James" hints that the humans who order the assassination of the alien are more dangerous to life than the alien itself. Very seldom did Simak ever portray the alien visitors as totally inimical; he was always wondering if their "invasion" could be a cry for help or an attempt to make contact with humanity. "The Golden Bugs" are aliens with a hive mind who invade suburbia and greedily gobble up all the metal in the neighborhood. The suburbanites drive off the invaders with ultrasonic waves, but even after the alien menace has been eliminated, the protagonist is torn with doubts if he has done the right thing. "...The first things from space had come and we had smashed them flat...Would the driving sense of fear and the unwillingness to understand bar all things from the stars?" (120).

When humans visit other planets their intent is to exploit the inhabitants in some way, but Simak lets the aliens fight back in non-violent, but ironically appropriate, ways. The alien punishment often fits the human crime. Earthlings hunt intelligent, telepathic Martians for fur and food in "Mirage" (*Amazing*, October 1950; original title, "Seven Came Back"). An archeologist, exiled in the desert by his crooked guides, makes friends with the Martians who treat him to a vision of a Martian New Jerusalem, a "shining city on Mars as it once was." When the guides arrive, they find the

mummified body of the archaeologist, but their glimpse of
the city is only a mirage.

A common pattern to these interplanetary adventures
is to have the survey expedition land and then not be able to
get home or have members of the expedition meet with an
inexplicable accident. In "Courtesy" (*Astounding Science
Fiction*, August 1951) the survey expedition is stricken with
a deadly virus to which the natives are immune. One of the
expedition members treats one of the natives with courtesy
(he stepped out of the native's path) and the natives cure him.
In "Beachhead" (original title, "You'll Never Go Home
Again," *Fantastic Adventures*, July 1951), a planetary survey
party is stranded when an alien virus destroys all the metal in
the spaceship. "Drop Dead" (*Galaxy*, June 1956) is the bitterly amusing story of an agricultural survey expedition
which lands on a planet populated by strange hybrids of
animal and vegetable called "critters." Critters are the perfect food; not only do they taste good but they conveniently
drop dead at your feet. Initially, the expedition is afraid to
eat critters. Then, the survey team runs low on food, and
there is nothing to do but eat critter. The consequences re-
call the injunction to Odysseus's men not to eat the cattle of
the god Helios, but in this case, when you eat critter, you become a critter—part of the perfect food chain of "you are
what you eat." NBC liked this story so much that it was
dramatized on their popular radio show, *X Minus One*.

An even more significant experience with off-world
aliens that expressed Simak's anti-war feelings awaits the
traders in "Retrograde Evolution" (*Science Fiction Plus*,
April 1953). A trading ship, hoping to pick up its cargo of
valuable *babu* root, finds no cargo waiting. An investigation
reveals that the natives have moved out of their villages and
are now living off the land. The natives have worked out an
ingenious way to keep from starting a war. Like Hari Seldon
in Asimov's *Foundation* series, they can predict a crisis point
statistically, and before such a point is reached, they insure
peace by deliberately retreating from progress. The expedition closes the planet to all visitors until this phenomenon
can be studied. Simak makes it terribly obvious that the

price of progress is war, at least in human terms, and the aliens have found a way out of the vicious cycle.

This same idea of being only as intelligent as necessary for survival is the theme of "The World That Couldn't Be" (*Galaxy*, January 1958). A planter on a planet filled with dangerous animals starts hunting a creature destroying his crops. When he catches up with the creature, he saves its life and learns that it is a planetary mother of whom all species of creatures on the planet are a part. The "mother" returns the favor and saves the planter's life but strikes a bargain with the planter complaining, "it is an awful effort to keep on being smart."

Simak also implies that, for all their apparent superiority, alien races have made some of the same mistakes as humankind. Like big brothers, those species who have experienced the difficult way to peace and brotherhood are trying to set humans on the same path. Simak's aliens use various methods to bring about this change, but the two most common are education and acceleration of the evolutionary process. The alien missionaries of "Kindergarten" (*Galaxy*, June 1953), observing Earth disguised as vending machines, set up a huge, invulnerable building on Peter Chaye's farm. (Chaye is dying of cancer, but the aliens cure him.) Peter and his girl friend feel compelled to enter the building. The military, making their customary paranoid response as if these aliens were Godzilla, unsuccessfully try to stop the couple by destroying the building with an atomic bomb. The huge building is a "school" for humanity, and Peter and Mary are among the first "pupils." The aliens have come to reform humanity by sending us back to school, and our "graduation" could lead to eventual acceptance into the brotherhood of the galaxy.

Instead of coming to Earth and risking armed opposition, Simak's aliens may reform humans by directing them to sources of universal knowledge. A group of greedy fortune hunters in "Jackpot" (*Galaxy*, October 1956) land their spaceship near a colossal miles-high, silo-shaped building. In the building, the looters find some "sticks" that can produce a living experience on another world. They have hit the jackpot, an entertainment that will make them all rich. An alien appears who tells them that the silo is a galactic university, specializing in home study and extension courses, with tests taken only every thousand years. As representatives of the human race, the crew may apply. The captain goes along with the alien, thinking of ways to exploit his find, but the scheme backfires when the crew takes the basic orientation course. The hunters no longer care to make a fast buck, have become "honorable and honest," and will take their knowledge back and turn it over to the authorities. Not all the humans are so easily converted, however; the captain and the ship's doctor refuse to take the course and go on hunting for the jackpot.

Someone in the galaxy, a council of races or a ruling Principle, must be responsible for setting up these libraries or repositories of knowledge for the education of inferior races like humanity. In "Junkyard" (*Galaxy*, May 1953) a planet-checking expedition comes upon a junkyard of alien equipment, evidence that another race has discovered space travel. In their investigations, they discover to their dismay that they have forgotten how to start the engines of their own spaceship and are marooned on the planet. They find some strange towers containing a creature, part animal and part machine. When they lower a human into the tower, he comes up a crying baby. The creatures are memory traps, which drain off knowledge and send it somewhere to a central receiver in the Galaxy. The crew reverses the "polarity" and knowledge pours out of the trap.

In "Immigrant" (*Astounding Science Fiction*, March 1954), Earthlings voluntarily travel to an alien world for their admittance into the brotherhood. One out of a thousand Earthlings are selected by the Kimonians, an alien humanoid race with parapsychic powers, to go to their planet. The planet Kimon is a "galactic El Dorado, a never-never land, the country at the rainbow's foot" (9). All Earthlings dream of going there and none ever wants to come back. An agent, selected to find out the secret of Kimon's attraction, is hired as a "pet" or playmate for the children of a Kimonian family. Other Earthlings on Kimon are kept happy by such delights as large bank accounts and "live-it" television (the agent actually "visits" the Battle of Hastings). In exchange, the

61

Earthlings are developing psi powers. The agent swallows his pride and accepts his inferiority, realizing that the Kimonians have allowed humans to emigrate to take the next step in human evolution.

In at least two stories, the results of alien control may not be so beneficial to humanity nor, as in "Jackpot," does the alien inoculation of values always take with every human. Human beings have already joined the galactic brotherhood in "The Civilization Game" (*Galaxy*, November 1958), and to keep their human culture intact, they set up the "Continuation" on Earth where old skills like politics and diplomacy or painting and music are still practiced to retain the knowledge of their manipulation and use. The protagonist is on the run because he played a game of dirty politics, and his opponents "dug up" assassination in response. He seeks asylum on his friend's estate. When the attempted assassination takes place, no one gets hurt, but the irony that human violence must be sublimated in a "civilized" game shows how thin the veneer of galactic influence really is.

In a very strange story that combines the themes of alien interference with the confusion of identity, "Final Gentleman" (*The Magazine of Fantasy & Science Fiction*, January 1960), a famous writer, the last surviving "gentleman," is phasing out his career. In a magazine interview occasioned by his retirement, he learns that certain facts about his life no longer seem to be true. When he goes to his mother's for dinner, he finds a stranger living there. Other evidence points to the fact that he is not really who he seems to be, that his gentleman's existence is imagined and not real. He has the ability to literally put himself in anyone else's situation by the power of his imagination. He remembers a deal he had made thirty years ago with a magazine book editor to play this double role to have influence on others who could drastically alter the course of world events.

The writer goes to the magazine as his shabbier real self for a showdown. At the magazine is "Harvey," a Jeanne-Dixon-like computer whose predictions have been amazingly right. The writer discovers that the editor is an alien who has been controlling humans (another "Harvey" was the Delphic oracle) but only at "crisis points" in human history. The writer becomes a Neanderthal and tears the alien apart; when he does, "Harvey" disappears. He concludes that humanity has a right and duty to be itself, without outside interference. The concept of "crisis points" in human history at which aliens appear and interfere in the course of human evolution is an idea that Simak will use in later novels, even as late as *Special Deliverance* (1982).

Such a story with a mixed reaction to alien intervention is not typical for Simak. In "Final Gentleman," Simak might have been more interested in playing with the idea of reality being created by human imagination, a theme he developed much better in other short stories like "Shadow Show" (see below). Simak's aliens, out of kindness and thoughtfulness and maybe self-protection, seem genuinely involved in finding solutions for human problems. In "New Folks Home" (*Astounding Science Fiction*, July 1963), aliens even go so far as to provide a place where the elderly can still be of service to the galaxy.

2. "THE BIG FRONT YARD"

Not all of Simak's aliens were interested in reforming the human race or bringing us free gifts. Some simply came to do business, to trade, and that brings us to one of Simak's most successful stories of the fifties, "The Big Front Yard." When this novella was first published in the October 1958 *Astounding*, it was an instant hit with the fans. (Simak had one of Kelly Freas's finest covers to accompany it.) "The Big Front Yard" easily won the 1959 Hugo for Best Novelette, and was later selected by the Science Fiction Writers of America as one of the greatest science-fiction novellas of all time and included in Ben Bova's *Science Fiction Hall of Fame, Volume Two-B*. No other story of Simak's has been more frequently collected except possibly for "Desertion" from the *City* sequence or "A Death in the House."

"The Big Front Yard" is a representative story, typical of the kind Simak had been writing since *City*, chock full of many familiar values, characters, and themes. It is difficult to account for its popular success because Simak had been writing the same, and occasionally better, alien encounter story all through the fifties. Perhaps the fans' attention had been focused on the Cold War problems too long, and they were looking for the peaceful economic solution to the problem of an alien invasion that the story offered.

Simak had touched earlier on this theme of aliens as traders in an amusing short story, "Dusty Zebra" (*Galaxy*, September 1954). An unseen Trader from another dimension leaves mysterious artifacts in the home of a middle-class suburban family. The family, anxious as most humans to make a buck off these gadgets but totally ignorant of their functions, trades some toy zebras for a miraculous dust collector. The dust collectors sell like hot cakes until the scheme backfires, and dust begins pouring back on this world—it seems the dust collectors had been siphoning off grime into an outraged *third* parallel universe.

Another story which might be an ancestor in direct line to "The Big Front Yard" is "Shadow World" (*Galaxy*, September 1957). An expedition is preparing an Earth-type planet for a colony. To prove they are adult members of the galactic community, the humans have come to the planet to start over, and not waste its natural resources, not "gut this world like man did Earth" (125). The expedition is falling behind schedule because their machines are constantly breaking down. The workers blame the Shadows, alien beings who have attached themselves to each man in the camp. The Shadows do not attempt to communicate with the humans, but merely hang around observing and are found to be making tiny models of everything in camp, including the humans. When one of the Shadows looks into a peeper, a forbidden device that can create fantasies dangerous enough to trap men's minds, the Shadow vanishes. Desperate because an inspector is coming to check up on their progress, the expedition tries to trap all the Shadows using the peeper. The humans conclude that the Shadows are alien proxies, machines to keep track of human activities. Another alien appears with life-size duplicates of everything in camp. He will deliver as many machines as they want, as long as the humans provide entertainment with the peeper. It does not look like the aliens are getting the better of the trade in "technologies," but then products of human imagination seem to have a high value in the galactic market.

In "The Big Front Yard" aliens also go to considerable trouble to start the bartering process. Hiram Taine—handyman, tinker, junk and antique dealer—and his faithful hound, Towser, awake one morning suspecting that some one or some thing is living in their house. His invisible guest has installed a ceiling of some impenetrable material in the basement, altered the television from black and white to color, and repaired the kitchen stove. Guided by Towser, Hiram and his half-witted friend, Beasley, dig up a milk-glass contraption in the woods. Beasley is one of Simak's "untouchables," the village outcast with miraculous powers; in this case, Beasley is telepathic (dogs can talk to him).

Returning from the woods that night, Hiram finds his front yard gone and in its place, a sunlit desert surrounding the house and stretching into the distance. Some rodent-like creatures come out of the front door and go marching off into the desert, obviously Hiram's uninvited guests who came in the milk-glass spaceship.

While Beasley runs to tell the town, Hiram sets off in his truck to explore this new world in his front yard. He finds more milk-glass vehicles and a house, whose back door leads into yet another world. This other world sends shivers down Hiram's spine...could it be one of the parallel Cobbly worlds Simak invented in *City*? Towser vanishes, but Hiram must return to get gas before he can search for his dog.

When Hiram gets back to the house, the whole world is in an uproar. The little town of Willow Bend has become international news: a greedy local banker wants to set up a land development company, the military wants to run "transport" through Hiram's house, and the United Nations and world governments are sending representatives.

Towser returns, conducting an alien who looks like a man-sized woodchuck, and three humanoids come riding up on anti-grav saddles. Beasley, who has been communicating telepathically with the woodchuck, tells Taine that the aliens want to trade ideas. At last, Hiram is on familiar territory and begins dickering with the aliens. When the representative from the U.N. shows up, Hiram has already made a deal to swap the concept of paint for the anti-grav saddles. The story ends with Hiram and Beasley offering to handle the trade agreements if the U.N. will keep Washington and the bigwigs from the other countries off their backs.

Once again, the small town hero triumphs over the power structures of the establishment. The two village outcasts, the half-wit and the junk man, are the only ones with the necessary cunning to barter with the aliens. Hiram, the shrewd Yankee trader, has put himself in the best bargaining position, and it looks like the aliens had planned it that way. They made no attempt to contact any government in the world—they came directly to the "little guys" to do business.

Simak has held inviolate another "frontier" value, "a man's home is his castle." Even in the face of such a momentous discovery, no authority has the right to usurp another's property. A person has the right to repel any and all intruders, especially if those intruders are government officials.

3. THE ROBOT STORIES

Scattered among all these many tales about aliens are a number of stories featuring sentient machines or robots. Simak was interested in the fate of robots and androids as human technology advanced and built better and better examples of artificial or machine intelligence. Should robots and androids be included in the brotherhood of intelligent life? For a long time, artificial beings, patterned on the Frankenstein and Rossum models, had also been getting a bad deal in science fiction. Asimov had improved their lot somewhat in his robot stories, but one of the stock science-fiction plots was to picture a robot as a creature of metal or synthetic flesh, without soul or emotion. Simak, in his *City* series, had humanized robots more by making them faithful retainers, loyal servants to the human race. He gave them Biblical names like Hezekiah, Abraham, or Ebenezer and in the latter days of the human race in *City*, Simak conceived wild robots setting up their own society and going off to the stars. But this Jeeves image showed robots with few feelings outside of loyalty and dedication. In the fifties and sixties,

Simak added a more "human" dimension to robots and gave them longings and desires more nearly akin to humans.

Robots had always been a source of humor in Simak's stories. "How-2" (*Galaxy*, November 1954) is a satirical treatment of robots and the do-it-yourself craze that swept the country in the fifties. By mistake, an ardent do-it-yourselfer receives a kit to assemble an experimental robot that can reproduce itself. The whole situation gets out of hand when the robots actually do reproduce, and the do-it-yourselfer gets involved in a lawsuit settled by declaring that robots have rights. The story is mildly amusing, raises some questions about whether intelligent machines are a curse or a blessing, but it is very surprising that such a light piece was chosen for Simak's debut on the Broadway stage.[7]

A funnier but sillier story than "How-2" is "Lulu" (*Galaxy*, June 1957). A fully automated spaceship christened Lulu falls in love with her human crew and "elopes" with them. Her data banks had been fed sentimental novels and bad poetry written by Jimmy, one of the crew. The crew tries to make Lulu angry by being inactive, one of the conditions a busy computer should hate. Lulu strikes back by landing herself on an Earth-type planet, fooling the crew, who all dash outside. (Lulu is programmed not to take off without members of the crew aboard.) The crew finds some ruins of an advanced civilization, containing some valuable artifacts, and are attacked by a strange beast, a "rhinoceros on wheels," a hybrid of biological and machine life dubbed Elmer, who Lulu says is after the phosphate in the crew's bones. When the crew protests at such treatment, Lulu reminds them, "...if there were metal in Elmer that humans wanted, you'd break him up without a second thought. That's the trouble with you and your human race" (36). To the crew's dismay, Lulu is "shacking up" with Elmer, and the two conspire to keep the crew away from the ruins. To break the stalemate, Jimmy, the bad poet, reads his "saga" to Lulu, a sucker for everything he writes. She boots Elmer out and takes off to "wander the starways." Jimmy is warned by the rest of the crew to write about the "comforts and glory of home."

Simak could also be deadly serious about robots and their feelings. Unlike the lovesick Lulu, another sentient spaceship picks up a marooned traveler in "The Shipshape Miracle" (*Worlds of If*, January 1963). The ship directs the traveler to his cabin and the walls start closing in. The ship needs a new brain; sighing in metallic contentment, it tells the traveler, "Finding you was a very miracle."

Simak's robots express their pathos best when they are afflicted by loneliness or the desire to be human. "Horrible Example" (*Astounding Science Fiction*, March 1961) starts out like a typical "poor village drunk" story. Tobias, the disgrace of Millville, is a drunken bum, a weight on the village conscience. Old Tobe is actually a robot, contracted to play the role of the one human derelict in town. Unworthily for a robot, he longs for "humanness" and to become a colonist among the stars. When he saves two kids in a car wreck, the village sends a delegation to make him a hero, and Tobe must send for a replacement "bum." Now Tobe will play a new role, a reformed bum who will make Millville nervous and uneasy—perhaps uneasy enough to send him to the stars.

The most daring in concept of these "lonely robot" stories is "All the Traps of Earth" (*The Magazine of Fantasy & Science Fiction*, March 1960). Simak not only elicits compassion for the robot protagonist's very human desire to retain his identity but continues a trend begun in *City* to have robots and androids start a new order of civilization. Rather than be reprogrammed, a six-hundred-year-old robot, Richard Daniel, disguises himself as human and stows away on a starship. When the starship takes off and goes into hyperspace, Richard is on the outside of the ship. Simak gives a marvelous description of Richard's thoughts and sensations in hyperspace—in most science-fiction stories, the occupants are inside and protected.

When Richard arrives on a planet run by robots, he "sees" a diagram of the spaceship, indicating that something is seriously wrong. Before he can issue any warning, the spaceship blows up. When another robot tries to kill him, he "sees" a diagram of the robot and turns him off. Richard has acquired these new abilities, apparently from his trip through hyperspace. He stows away again on a ship bound for the planet Arcadia, a pastoral paradise and duplicate of Earth. On the journey, Richard wonders why he, a robot, has been granted the gift of paranormal ability instead of a human being. Arcadia needs Richard—to cure a sick child, to fix a broken appliance, or perhaps to teach the people his special talents.

Maybe it had all been planned to work out this way:

> If the human race could not attain directly the paranormal power he held, this instinct of the mind, then they would gain it indirectly through the agency of one of their creations (159).

Richard has avoided all the traps of Earth to gain his freedom except the last—true to his kind, he must use his gift for the service of humanity.

Although stories about aliens and robots dominated his output from the fifties to the middle sixties, Simak did turn his attention to other issues. He played with future history scenarios somewhat different from *City*, but none of these stories has much lasting value. "Worlds Without End" (*Future*, Winter 1956-57) is an adventure story, a power struggle among unions or guilds who make up a government by committee (the most powerful guild provides century-long dreams for those in suspended animation). "Full Cycle" (*Original Science Fiction Stories*, November 1955) is almost an exact repetition of the *City* theme but with a more optimistic outcome for the human race. The people have deserted the cities, returned to a nomadic form of life, and civilization has gone "full cycle," tribe to city and city back to tribe. Psi powers, repressed and ignored in the triumph of machines, are developed as a substitute. An old man, a historian whose occupation is now obsolete, finds a new mission in teaching the tribes about their emerging abilities. Simak will develop this paranormal solution to human problems better in later novels like *Time Is the Simplest Thing* (see below).

ROBERT J. EWALD

Simak also tried his hand at the generation spaceship theme in "Target Generation" (*Science Fiction Plus*, August 1953, originally "Space-Bred Generations"). The surviving generations think of the ship as a world, not a mode of transport. The Myth and the Legend of the Ship have become a meaningless religion with "holy pictures" of Trees and Sky and Clouds, and knowledge has been suppressed. The story takes place at the Beginning of the End, when the ship rights itself preparatory to landing. The protagonist acquires the knowledge necessary to land the ship but must reintroduce killing, an outlawed act, to protect this knowledge and save the lives of the others.

An ancient philosophical question that Simak liked to ask and answer metaphorically was—does reality have an independent existence or is it only the creation of our minds? A later novel *Out of Their Minds* (1970) plays outrageously with this idea, but Simak first introduced it in short stories. An early effort was one of his few collaborations, "The Street That Wasn't There" (*Comet Stories*, July 1941), written with Carl Jacobi.[8] In this fantasy, a recluse philosophy professor wakes up to see signs that the world is losing its population through war and plague. He had once speculated that all that holds the world together is the power of the human mind and that some stronger intelligence from another dimension could reach out and steal our universe out from under us. The story has a *Weird Tales* ending—a gray fog obscures the world outside and a colossal face of immense power and evil is swallowing up our living space.

Two stories on the same theme with less unsettling consequences are "Founding Father" (*Galaxy*, April 1957) and "Shadow Show" (*The Magazine of Fantasy & Science Fiction*, November 1953). The hero of "Founding Father" is a mutant immortal who lands on a planet to found a colony after a century in space. To preserve his sanity on the trip, Earthlings provided him with a *dimensino*, a machine that deluded him with imaginary companions to pass the time. Winston cannot totally dispel the illusion even after his robots tell him the truth. The story ends ambiguously: "He heard steps on the stairway, the sound of many happy, friendly voices, coming up to get him" (74).

70

"Shadow Show" mingles the conflict of reality versus illusion with the guilt caused by technology. A group of nine biologists has been isolated on an asteroid, attempting to create beings who can survive on other planets. Earthlings must be "strong" when they encounter other intelligences. The group is oppressed by guilt over their activities, compounding the psychological problems of isolation. To amuse themselves and remain sane, they put on a Play in which each member of the group imagines a character in a continuing drama displayed on a screen, like a television soap opera.

When the story opens, one of the team in opposition to the project has just died, but the identity of the character he created is unknown to the rest of the group. When they again begin to play the drama, however, all the nine characters are present, which gives rise to all kinds of speculations: who is Character Number Nine? Is it a bad joke? Is the machine itself sentient? Or is Henry a ghost? Finally, Henry's character is unmasked as the Philosopher, the most assertive character in the play, and the mystery is solved.

The characters have taken on lives of their own, playing out their parts without humans pulling the strings, but life has gone out of the team, their dedication burned out by fear, conflict, and death. Ironically, by the power of mind and electronics, the group has succeeded in creating life. They failed at their work but triumphed at their play. The guilt that plagued Frankenstein and other scientists who created life in the laboratory is not necessary—no more monsters to destroy before they get loose—just sit before a screen and dream them up.

There is no question that Simak had served his "apprenticeship" in the short-story form. His newspaper experience had made him master of the "hook" to capture the reader's attention; he knew how to blend moral seriousness, humor, and human interest in a pleasing mixture to keep the reader around; and he had mastered the ironic, surprise ending to send readers away feeling that they had read a good science-fiction story. In addition, most of the motifs that Simak experimented with in these three-score-plus short stories written during this maturation period of fifteen years would provide the basis of his longer works in the next twenty years. After 1963 Simak would become a full-time novel writer and, with some exceptions, he would never again produce short stories in this quality and quantity again.

4. THE FIRST NOVELS: *TIME AND AGAIN*

Before 1950 Simak had written only one novel that was actually his own invention, the space opera *The Cosmic Engineers*. Although *The Cosmic Engineers* had what fans liked to call "sweep" and was brimming with ideas, Simak was only experimenting with a form of science fiction that was popular in 1939. It remained to be seen if Simak could sustain his own style in a longer work. When H. L. Gold chose *Time and Again* (originally serialized as *Time Quarry*) to be the lead story in his new magazine *Galaxy*, he insured the success of Simak's venture as a novelist. And for complicated plots, Simak's second novel holds second place to no one; events occur with van Vogtian suddenness.

The setting of the novel is 7980 A.D., when humanity, spread thinly throughout the galaxy, has established an empire held together by ruthlessness and aggression, even though violence is expressly forbidden except for dueling. Asher Sutton returns to Earth after being killed in a crash-landing on one of the unknown planets of 61 Cygni, restored to life by its inhabitants. He vaguely describes these aliens as "symbiotic abstractions," and his mind has fused with one of the beings Sutton calls Johnny and who describes itself as Sutton's "destiny." Sutton has acquired superhuman abilities, powers demonstrated by his journey from Cygni without air or food in a wrecked ship. He has other superhuman attributes: two hearts, an extra circulatory system, and extraordinary psi powers—using only his mind, he can kill, fly a ship, heal his own body, or read another person's mind and feelings. Adams, Sutton's boss, is warned by a man from the future that Sutton must be killed before he can write a book entitled *This Is Destiny*, which will profoundly change the universe.

Several factions contest to keep Sutton from finishing the book: the Revisionists of Sutton's book, men from the future who want to maintain human superiority; Adams, who

fears Sutton will bring a return to violence; and the Android
Equality League, headed by the girl Eva, who is in love with
Sutton and who wants the equality of all intelligent life. To
escape the machinations of all these groups, Sutton fights a
duel, revives from being killed by men from the future, then
jumps six-thousand years into the past after finding a letter
from his ancestor describing the visit of a time traveler from
the future. His ancestor, of course, lives in Bridgeport, Wisconsin, Simak's favorite stomping ground, and Simak takes a
breather from the breakneck action by giving Sutton ten
years of peace in a rural setting. When Sutton returns from
the past, he joins forces with Eva and the androids, who help
him to escape Earth to write his book.

The message of Sutton's book is simple and reiterates
the brotherhood of intelligent life:

We are not alone.
No one is ever alone.
Not since the first faint stirring of the first
flicker of life on the first planet in the galaxy
that knew the quickening of life, has there
ever been a single entity that walked or
crawled or slithered down the path of life
alone (Chapter 20).

Sutton, of all the forms of life, was let through to
Cygni to carry the truth back to the galaxy: all life is a symbiosis. Each living thing has free will, yet has a "destiny," a
"parasite" to which the "host" can listen or respond if it
wants to, and evolution is the result of this "conversation."
In exchange, the "destiny" attains a semblance of life it could
not have independently. Sutton's paranormal abilities are the
product of his symbiosis with Johnny.

In one neat package, Simak ties together the problems of God, fate, and evolution, and attaches a purpose to
intelligence. Humanity can no longer maintain the self-
delusion of superiority in the wake of this revelation, and
even androids, now fully living things who have discovered
how to reproduce themselves, can cast away their inferiority.
One of the human race has been chosen as a galactic Messiah

and granted superhuman powers to write a new divine revelation, the Bible of the brotherhood of intelligent life. Simak lays the burden of the choice on the aliens of 61 Cygni but leaves room for speculation that there may be some other universal Principle at work behind the plan.

5. *RING AROUND THE SUN*

Simak's second published novel in the fifties was *City*, but this novel was actually not based on new material but on a linked series of short stories written in the forties. He published another new novel in *Galaxy* (December 1952-February 1953), *Ring Around the Sun*, which continued the theme of the alien brotherhood correcting the ills of humankind, but also enabled Simak to take a potshot at the business establishment.

Simak proved again that he could write complex plots. It is the year 1987, the cold war is still on, but a more serious threat to the world economy has appeared. Somebody is selling at ridiculously low prices such consumer goods as cars that run forever, razor blades that never dull, light bulbs that never dim, and houses heated by cheap solar energy. This same mysterious industry is giving away synthetic carbohydrates to starving populations. A writer, Jay Vickers, is summoned to New York by his agent, Ann Carter, to meet a man named Crawford, representing the industrial combine. The combine is naturally upset at such a threat to conspicuous consumption and planned obsolescence. Crawford wants Vickers to write a book, "impartially" explaining what is happening, but Vickers is not interested.

The thought of home makes Vickers think about his life. Vickers has always been "different," and other people sense his difference. He recalls an incident from his childhood when he spun a top and followed the swirling streaks into "Fairyland." On the run from an angry mob, which thinks he did away with his neighbor Flanders, Vickers flees in one of the Forever cars. Crawford reappears and informs Vickers that Vickers is a latent mutant. Meanwhile, the populace has reacted with mob violence to the new gadgets, and world leaders keep the violence inflamed by blaming a mutant plot to take over the world. Vickers spins a top and escapes into Fairyland, an alternate world named Earth 2. He heads for home (at the junction of the Wisconsin and Mississippi Rivers—where else?) and, on the way, stumbles on a completely automated factory where the Forever cars are made. When he arrives, Vickers is shocked to overhear that he and Ann are both androids.

Jay has figured out the mutants' master plan. To re-build a culture gone wrong, mutants are reshaping the human race by taking away their "deadly toys," destroying their economy, and transporting them to alternate worlds to start a new Utopian society where war and fear would be outlawed. On Earth 2, society is at the pastoral-feudal stage, a time to re-establish the common touch between humanity and the land. (The novel's title comes from the concept of a string of such alternate Earths circling the sun just one second apart.) The mutants have carried on a secret existence down through the ages and have formed groups who can "listen to the stars" and catch the thoughts of other intelligent creatures. To increase their manpower, mutants are capable of dividing their "essence" among several android bodies. (Simak care-fully avoided dealing with the grave conflicts such a split personality could cause, but after all, mutants could probably handle it.)

Vickers meets Flanders, who tells Jay that he was removed from his mutant human body at age eighteen and put in an android body. Flanders and a third android, whose identity Flanders will not reveal, are also parts of the original Jay Vickers. Jay believes the third android is Ann, with whom he is in love. Jay has the inherent ability to make hunches (an idea Simak borrowed from "Hunch" [1943], one of his earlier short stories), and his job is to use this ability to stop Crawford. Crawford is planning to start a limited war, allowing governments to control their economies and stop the flow of mutant gadgets. As a reward, Jay will be re-turned to his youthful human body. The mutants are now working on immortality, and Jay's parents, in suspended animation for cooperating with the mutants, are awaiting this gift.

Jay returns to our Earth and picks up Ann. Ann is a telepath, and Jay's worst suspicions are now confirmed. Jay arranges to meet Crawford and his board of directors and sends the board into an alternate world, effectively stopping Crawford's plans. During this process, Crawford remembers his own childhood trip to Fairyland. Crawford is the third Vickers android, not Ann.

In *Ring Around the Sun* Simak was very critical of the industrial complex and severely indicted the present technological culture. Instead of a gentle complaint as in *City*, he bitterly attacked the conformity and callousness of the nuclear age:

> ...a culture founded on a hatred and a terrible pride and a suspicion of everyone who did not talk the same language or eat the same food or dress the same as you did....
>
> It was a lopsided mechanical culture of clanking machines, a technological world that could provide creature comfort, but not human justice or security.... It had concentrated upon the technological and had ignored the sociological so that a man might punch a button and destroy a distant city without knowing, or even caring, about the lives and habits, the thoughts and hopes and beliefs of the people that he killed (Chapter 43).

Such a society would react violently to an invented mutant menace and burn the shops where the gadgets designed to help humanity are sold. The only choice the mutants have is to break down the whole rotten structure of society and ship the pieces off to an alternate world. The concept of using an alternate world as a dumping ground for the human race is directly borrowed from *City*, but in this future, Simak offers the hope of starting over and doing better the next time. The mutants have compassion for their fellow humans and are willing to help those worth saving to overcome their violence and prejudice, unlike the mutant Joe in *City*, who was totally uncaring and turned his attention to improving the lot of the ants. The mutants have accelerated their plan by "listening to the stars" and receiving help from other alien races. Simak did not develop this idea of alien help at all in the novel, but the presence of the brotherhood is clearly in the background.

6. *TIME IS THE SIMPLEST THING*

When Simak started writing novels steadily in 1961 after a nine-year hiatus, he returned to the alien brotherhood theme. In the 1961 *Time Is the Simplest Thing*, originally serialized as *The Fisherman* (*Analog*, April-July 1961), aliens again help humans to move up the evolutionary ladder. The novel may be read as a defense of the civil rights of parapsychic mutants, but their new freedom is gained only with the help of the hero traveling telepathically to the stars and bringing back an alien mind. An ageless, grotesque creature simply called the "Pinkness" fuses with the mind of the hero, Shepherd Blaine, giving Blaine the additional power to travel in time. Blaine philosophizes fraternally to the Pinkness, "You're just a blob of life—brother to everything that ever existed or ever will exist" (Chapter 9).

Blaine is an explorer for Fishhook, an organization that brings back commodities from the stars and is systematically destroying capitalism for its own self-interest. Since Blaine has "gone alien" and acquired more advanced psi powers, Fishhook wants to eliminate him, but Blaine throws in with the "parries," short for paranormal human beings, who are fighting for their lives against the witch hunts of the "normals." The rest of the novel is the story of Blaine's efforts to escape and defeat Fishhook, who wants to maintain a monopoly on paranormal powers, and his involvement with the parry movement to advance all of humanity. The paranormals are themselves divided into those who want to start over with a pastoral paradise somewhere among the stars and those who only see "evil in the stars." Blaine comes up with a solution; the parries can go, body and mind, to other planets and start their own Edens, making Fishhook obsolete.

Simak was always fascinated with the nature of time, and the novel contains some eerie descriptions of traveling in time. When Blaine goes into the past with the help of the Pinkness, the past is a dead place of shadows of all solid things. The Earth existed "through every point in time, a sort of limited eternity to provide a solid matrix" (Chapter 11). But all else is ghosts—fences, trees, farms, bridges—shadows of the present, persisting in the past.

The novel is a serious apology for the civil rights of paranormals (or any other minority group) and repeats some conventions that Simak used over and over: mutants with psi powers including telepathic travel to the stars ignoring the faster-than-light limitation, telepathic contact with alien intelligences over vast distances, and an explanation of supernatural events as psi phenomena.

7. *THEY WALKED LIKE MEN*

Simak tried something different with aliens in 1962 with *They Walked Like Men*, an original Doubleday hardcover not serialized previously anywhere, and Simak's first departure from magazine publication. The aliens are the old-fashioned uncaring nasty kind, but instead of using laser rays or man-eating plants to wipe us out, they plan to conquer by economics. The novel follows the format of a thriller, and Simak brings back his newspaperman hero to solve the mystery. In the first chapter, the newsman is nearly caught in a vicious human-trap, actually one of the shape-changing aliens, who naturally look like black bowling balls. (Simak always referred to this novel in interviews as that "bowling ball" story.) The reporter, with the help of his girl friend, tumbles on to the aliens' scheme to send the world into economic chaos: if aliens own all the property and property rights vanish, it will be an end to jobs, credit, and business—and, of course, to the hopes and dreams of humanity.

The aliens are succeeding because of their incredible metamorphic ability—they change into such exact replicas of humans that no one can tell the difference. They are totally unfeeling galactic realtors, buying and selling planets, unconcerned about the races inhabiting them. Nobody will believe in such an invasion, and the situation looks hopeless until the newsman hero discovers that the odor of skunks distracts the aliens like sex does for humans. The news hawk sniffs out Windy, an old skunk handler and one of Simak's unlikely saviors of the human race, who rounds up enough skunks to halt the invasion.

The solution to the alien problem is absolutely silly but pure Simak. Simak admitted that one of his basic story-telling ploys was to toss in humor when serious emotions became too strong. In fact, the whole story is almost a put-on of Jack Finney's *The Invasion of the Body Snatchers*, the aliens taking on the form of humans but without the horror of Finney's creations. Also, the idea that aliens might destroy the fabric of capitalism by undermining property rights did not disturb Simak very much. *They Walked Like Men* is an entertainment, but underneath the fun was Simak shaking his finger at the human race, and especially America, for its sin-gle-minded reliance on free enterprise.

8. *WAY STATION*

In his next novel, Simak returned to his favorite theme, the brotherhood of the galaxy. This time Simak posed a more difficult question: can humanity, by its *own* efforts, become a member of the brotherhood? If the human mania for technology is driving toward catastrophe and mo-rality has declined so far that alien visitors are prompted to attempt a reform, what chance does humanity have to take its place in the galactic brotherhood of intelligent life? How can such an unworthy species as the human race ever be-come deserving of joining other intelligent races in a com-mon quest?

Simak came up with a possible answer in his 1963 novel *Way Station*, first published as *Here Gather the Stars* in *Galaxy* (June-August 1963). When *Way Station* first ap-peared in book form, it was not an instant success. P. Schuyler Miller was the only one to unequivocally praise it in his review column.[9] Other critics admired the skill with which Simak handled its major elements, but did not rank the novel with *City*.

But a cool critical reception did not keep the fans from granting *Way Station* the Hugo award as the best novel of 1963. And time has only proven that *Way Station*, despite a slightly flawed ending, is without question one of Simak's most enduring works. It deals with cosmic concepts so large that they span the galaxy, yet Simak kept it all in perspective by focusing all the action within a few square miles around a farmhouse near his favorite spot, the confluence of the Wisconsin and the Mississippi Rivers.

The action also centers around the struggle within the soul of one lonely, troubled man, Enoch Wallace. Enoch Wallace, born in 1840 and a veteran of the Civil War, must be 120 years old—yet to all outside appearances, he looks only thirty years old. He lives in the old family farmhouse, only venturing outside an hour a day and communicating with no one but the mailman and a sensitive deaf-mute, Lucy Fisher. The country folk have long accepted him as a local oddity, but recently Enoch has attracted the attention of U.S. Intelligence.

Enoch is actually the keeper of a Way Station for beings from all over the galaxy to travel from one place to another (the image of a stagecoach way station comes to mind). Because Earth is considered too backward to join the galactic community, the station must operate in secret. As long as Enoch remains within the house where time stands still, he never ages. The gift of immortality is his compensation for isolating himself from the rest of his world. In addition, Enoch has the unique opportunity to converse with exotic beings from all over the galaxy. Enoch nurtures the hope that someday Earth will be admitted to the galactic brotherhood.

Despite the excitement of his job, Enoch is very unhappy. Long ago in desperation, he used some alien magic to "create" some shadow people of his own (Simak introduced this ability in his 1953 novella "Shadow Show"), and one of these shadow people is the beautiful Mary, with whom he has gradually fallen in love. In a way, Mary symbolizes his greater plight, for his whole existence is a shadow; Enoch dares not touch the real world for fear of finding that *he* has become unreal.

But like it or not, the real world encroaches on Enoch's privacy. Intelligence agent Claude Lewis is intent on discovering Enoch's secret, Lucy Fisher has taken refuge in the Way Station from her brutal father, and Earth is headed toward nuclear holocaust, the customary Simakian destiny for the human race. Enoch would like to use knowledge from his alien contacts to relieve the situation, but to do so would betray Galactic Central and his boss and closest friend, Ulysses.

All is not well in the Galaxy, either. A basic Force (oh, the debt George Lucas owes to the science-fiction community!), focused through a mechanism called the Talisman, once moderated conflict in galactic society, but now the Talisman has been gone for many years. Factionalism has crept into the galactic brotherhood, and agent Lewis, by his tampering in the station, has turned the galaxy against Earth.

Enoch is caught in a conflict of loyalties, and his tortured soul becomes the cauldron in which this crisis in galactic relations is bubbling. Even his ghost friends desert him and flee back into the shadows. Enoch has many hard choices, not the least of which is Ulysses's method to stop the impending holocaust—Earth's people can be made to forget all they know about technology for several generations (we know from previous works that Simak thought this was not such a bad idea). Conditions reach a stalemate, a frequent crisis point in Simak's novels.

If there is any fault in *Way Station*, it is the *deus ex machina* Simak cranked down to resolve Enoch's dilemma. The being who stole the Talisman tries to hide out on Earth by traveling through the Way Station. Enoch kills him, and Lucy Fisher becomes the new custodian of the Talisman. All the loose ends are then tied up: the planet that sired the new custodian could scarcely be denied admittance to the galactic fraternity; Enoch's secret can be revealed; contact with other races will defuse the political powder keg on Earth; and the galaxy has its Talisman back. All the races of the galaxy can now live in brotherhood happily ever after.

Such an ending might be considered both emotionally and dramatically unsatisfying. Simak emulated Euripides by resolving the impossible situation with the improbable coincidence of the appearance of the alien thief. But who cares?—what novelist has not found it necessary to use coincidence to move the plot along? Through Earth's dilemma, readers are made aware of the harsh choices that individuals must make—choices which often must be made out of self-doubt, loneliness, or conflicting loyalties. Enoch Wallace is able to make the choice because he is among Simak's elect—one of Simak's truly moral men. But it is the ultimate irony of the ending that far overshadows the mechanism used to bring it into being. Without the intercession of the Talisman, non-human intelligences will lose their ability to live in peace—yet it is unworthy humanity that saves the galaxy from the same destruction allotted to Earth.

9. ALL FLESH IS GRASS

Before closing this chapter and turning our attention to Simak's novels in the late sixties, we should discuss one more of Simak's "alien invasion" novels in this context, *All Flesh Is Grass* (1965), which was nominated for a Nebula and was runner-up for Best Novel. In 1964 and 1965, Simak wrote very little fiction, two short stories and one novel; he devoted a lot of his time to writing non-fiction and even edited a collection of essays on modern science.[10]

All Flesh Is Grass centers all of its action in the little town of Millville, and most of the story is told through the thoughts and actions of the small town. The unlikely hero, Brad Carter, is an unsuccessful realtor who aspired to be an artist but stayed on in Millville, a failure in the eyes of the town. Strange things are happening in Millville—someone has erected an invisible barrier around the town and only inanimate objects can move in or out, voices come over cordless and dial-less telephones, and the village idiot, Tupper, who vanished ten years ago, reappears in Carter's backyard, "naked as a jaybird." The only connection Brad can make among these events is some purple flowers grown in his father's greenhouse.

The residents of Millville are in a panic and suspicious of Brad. Suddenly, the barrier moves, stripping the soil bare, and a storm of seeds descends on the bare ground. Tupper disappears again, and Carter follows Tupper's trail into an alternate world where the purple flowers cover everything. The flowers, an alien group mind, are running out of living space and want to make a deal with the human race. In exchange for more *lebensraum*, the flowers will provide Earth with food, shelter, and best of all, their accumulated knowledge. The flowers explain that they had often been in contact with many minds on Earth—could they be responsible for humanity's achievements? Brad is uneasy about the flowers' offer, especially after he finds some human bones.

Brad returns to Millville and tries to get the authorities to believe his story (the military and the Feds have now arrived). As a goodwill gift and a demonstration of their powers, the flowers grow fifty-dollar bills on trees in Brad's garden. The flowers have one other very specific condition—the human race must banish nuclear war. Radiation is the one danger the flowers fear.

The story reaches the inevitable Simak stalemate: will the flowers continue to take over the Earth, or will the government drop an atomic bomb on Millville to stop the flowers? Stiffy, the town bum, turns up with the answer. Despite the incredible age and knowledge of the flowers, no other race but humans has ever grown them and appreciated their beauty.

Like *Way Station, All Flesh Is Grass* concentrates events that affect the life of the whole planet in the microcosm of the small town of Millville. What Millville decides determines the future of the human race. The Millville community is full of ordinary people faced with an extraordinary situation. Are the people of Millville with their provincial prejudices and insular narrow-mindedness capable of the moral judgments necessary to negotiate an agreement with an alien race? In the end, the town is saved by those least likely to save it: a self-confessed failure, the village drunk, and the village idiot. The aliens can only communicate with those who are "different," never the "solid" citizens who turn out to be bigots and hardheads directing their fears and frustrations at those who might save them.

Also, as in *Way Station*, the ending may be too contrived, too sentimental for many readers. The concept that alien invaders are flowers who can be coerced because humanity loves their beauty may be a bit hard to swallow, but

Simak is to be admired for daring to present such a solution. Violence was the usual way of dealing with invaders.

All Flesh Is Grass is a suitable place to end a period in Simak's career in which he affirmed certain specific themes over and over again with appropriate variations—all themes that Simak had begun to use in his earlier fiction. He vented his frustrations with the direction the human race is taking—its blind use of technology steering a course towards self-destruction guided by the greed of big business. He established the presence of a community of intelligent life in the universe; a goal for the human race was admittance to this community, but only after humanity had changed its ways. Inherently, the human race had potential for greatness; Simak imagined humans as evolving psi powers so powerful that they could teleport themselves to the stars. However, to develop this potential, humans need help from the galactic community, and only certain humans, with the necessary moral strength and unselfish concern, are qualified to receive this help. Frequently, these selected humans are among society's unfortunates—the misfits, drunks, idiots, and losers.

Simak would use these same patterns in his later fiction but would add fantasy elements not in strict accordance with the rules of "hard" science fiction. When writers from the New Wave were triggering either disgust or uncensored approbation from the fans, his work from the late sixties to the early seventies would be variously labeled as "zany" or "kitsch" or even "speculative smog."

V.

THE ZANY SIMAK

By 1967, when science fiction was being inundated by the New Wave, Simak had attained solid success as a science-fiction writer, but not enough for him to desert the newspaper business and turn full-time writer. By 1966 he was ranked seventh in a poll conducted by P. Schuyler Miller among 414 *Analog* readers. In the same year, readers voted for their favorite all-time science-fiction book, and *City* ranked number nine (the *Foundation* series was first). In a similar poll in 1956, *City* had been rated number two, just under J. Francis McComas and Raymond J. Healy's *Adventures in Time and Space*.[1]

With the publication of *The Werewolf Principle* (1967) and *The Goblin Reservation* (1968), Simak's work began to exhibit a change that Muriel Becker dubbed "zany,"[2] but what is really only Simak extending a tendency that had always appeared in his work, even in *City*. He began mixing traditional fantasy elements with traditional science-fiction themes, mingling "ghosts with robots." Some readers and critics objected loudly to this contamination by one of their favorite science-fiction authors. In response, Simak claimed he never felt that science fiction had to be absolutely based on science and never considered himself a "hard science" writer. He could not understand why the development of imaginative literature should be limited by "the narrow bounds of what might be called classical science fiction." He agreed that science fiction is the source of a modern mythology, and he saw no reason why such "old and new mythologies cannot be successfully interweaved.... Goblins are expected to be found in ruined castles; they could be found with as much effect in an Iowa barn."[3]

Many of these "fantasy" themes were holdovers from Simak's work in the fifties. Simak had long ago given up the mainstay of all science-fiction adventure—the space ship. More and more, his space travelers teleported themselves to other stars; and no radio-telescopes for his characters—they communicated with aliens by "listening" to the stars. He had always allowed his characters to shuffle off to alternate worlds and dimensions at will, and many of the supernatural beings like goblins, ghosts, and ghouls were simply aliens who came to Earth a long time ago and became the stuff of folktales.[4]

1. *WHY CALL THEM BACK FROM HEAVEN?*

But simultaneously with these more unconventional stories, Simak wrote a novel as fresh as today's newspaper, which dramatized the problems raised by "cryogenics" or "cryonics," the fad of freezing corpses or terminally ill people to preserve them until such a time when medical science discovers cures for all ills or the power to resurrect the dead. In 1967 the Cryonics Society of California froze several newly dead people, and in the same year, Doubleday published Simak's *Why Call Them Back from Heaven?*

In this future history, Simak imagines the world of 2148 A.D. in a state of constant hopefulness, waiting for the gift of immortality. In ten years Forever Center will make that dream come true, or so it promises. Despite technological advances, almost everyone is living in self-imposed poverty to buy Forever stock and investments for the future, while Forever Center, with the accumulated wealth of two centuries, has become more powerful than most of the world's governments. Some dissenters to this new dream of living forever are causing the Center problems: the Holies, an organized religious opposition whose motto is the title of the book, and the Loafers, a small population who roam freely in bands eking out a living. Space travel has not located any habitable living space for the ninety-six billion applicants for revival, and time travel will be a necessity to relieve the coming population explosion. Mona Campbell, one of the time travel researchers, was close to a solution using alien mathematics, but she has disappeared.

The plot centers around Daniel Frost, head of public relations for the Center, who stumbled on a piece of paper from a confidential file, which might be evidence that Forever Center is a fraud, a scheme dreamed up to end war. Frost is framed and ostracized from his fellow humans by the security chief at Forever Center, except for his lawyer girl friend Ann. Fleeing for his life, Frost returns to his home town of Bridgeport, Wisconsin, where he finds Mona Campbell. Mona has found a new hope for a better second life, but not what Forever Center has been promising for the last two-hundred years. Death is a translation to another form; life and death are like matter and energy and cannot be destroyed, only changed to another form, "the law of the conservation of life." Mona cannot reveal this truth—it would make fools of all mankind.

After this revelation, the ending is anti-climactic. The confidential secret that nearly gets Dan killed turns out to be the sordid fact that the security chief was embezzling funds from the Center.

Despite its faults and mixed reviews—Algis Budrys called the plot a "simpleminded chase"[5] and Judith Merril remarked on the "provocative, though sketchy conclusion"[6]—the novel is a gentle satire on the search for eternal life and explores whether immortality can be found by faith in science or by faith in God. Simak examined this question by shifting the point of view away from Frost's problems, which are simple action-adventure-chase, and following the spiritual progress of other characters: a man, now seeking his immortality in the church, unfairly condemned by a mechanical jury to lose his own chance for preservation for not picking up a corpse on time; a greedy old man on a treasure hunt to recover a fortune in jade to make him millions in his future life; a religious zealot seeking the "truth" through prayer, fasting, and wandering through the wilderness; and Mona Campbell, a heroine who ironically possesses the truth but conceals it to protect the world. The book closes with doubts about the fate of humanity and Forever Center. Simak again turned his back on religious faith as the answer:

"Faith was never more, even at the best, than the implied hope for evidence" (Chapter 36). And a more searing condemnation is the religious zealot's total loss of faith in the final lines of the book: "There was never more than one way and now it doesn't work...We have been abandoned...God has turned his back on us" (Chapter 37).

The theme of the consequences of becoming immortal was always in the back of Simak's mind. As long ago as 1949 in "Eternity Lost" (*Astounding Science Fiction*, July), Simak was concerned about having enough room for all the people when immortality becomes a reality. When pioneers are sent to the stars in this story, they are granted the gift of immortality, while others remaining on Earth (if worthy of the privilege) merely have their lives extended. An ingenious solution to the emotional problems of being immortal is found in "Second Childhood" (*Galaxy*, February 1951). Immortality is not a blessing to Andrew Young, 5786 years old. He is lonely, tired, and as he grows older, instead of forgetting, his memories grow sharper. Suicide is outlawed, and Young's petition to end his life is denied by the authorities. In desperation, Young forces his mind to return to infancy, has a house and furnishings built giant-size, and even has an android built as a substitute Mommy. He has hit on the perfect relief valve for future immortals—repeat the life cycle. Stated so baldly, the plot seems inane, yet this story contains some of Simak's finest and most sensitive writing, especially those passages describing Young's feelings at becoming a child again.

2. *THE WEREWOLF PRINCIPLE*

Uncharacteristically, Simak skipped a year and published two novels in 1967. In this second novel, *The Werewolf Principle*, Simak was back on familiar ground, humanity's relationship to the inhabited universe. In the world of 2487 A.D. bioengineers have developed androids who can change into alien species, take up the life of an alien creature, and then revert back to human form. Andrew Blake, one of these experimental androids, assumed two such alien forms, complete with alien intellect and alien emotions. One is called Thinker, a logical mind in pyramidal shape that feeds on pure energy; the other is Quester, a telepath in wolf shape who can receive pictures sent out by alien intelligences. But something goes wrong and Blake's mind is not wiped clean of each alien presence. Blake, called Changer by the other two, has become a trinity of multiple beings all occupying the same body simultaneously, capable of changing into three different bodies at will.

When Blake is found frozen in a space capsule orbiting an asteroid in the Antares star system, his memory is blank except for general information about Earth two hundred years ago. Blake, searching for his identity, is helped by the telepathic Brownies, migrant alien psychologists who have been studying Earth for ages, and by a senator, a proponent of bioengineering for space colonization. Believing himself human, Blake falls in love with the senator's daughter, Elaine.

When Blake finally realizes who he is, he follows a message to Willow Grove, and the sight of the town jogs his memory. He remembers that his mind is that of a real human being, physicist Teddy Roberts, impressed upon his synthetic brain. Pursued by the humans who think he is a werewolf, Blake is depressed by his alienness. He is a monster, a freak, yet part of him longs for human love.

> Earth wanted to get rid of him, perhaps afraid of him, perhaps merely disgusted by him, a loathsome product of its own ambitions and imagination that must be quickly swept underneath the rug. For there was no place for him on the Earth or in humanity and yet he was a human product .... (Chapter 33)

Blake remains in the Willow Grove cemetery chapel for a year, in the shape of Thinker who begins collecting data to solve the riddle of the Universe. Blake becomes both an object of curiosity and a Messiah to a religious cult. Changer finally returns against the wishes of the other two, which pinpoints his identity crisis: even if he wanted to remain human, does he have the right because of the other two?

With the help of the Brownies, Earth proposes a solution to the problem of Blake. He will be sent out on a quest, an immortal body in an immortal ship, to put his triple being and tripled special powers to work seeking out the mind that "operates the Universe—that pushes all the necessary buttons." Rejected by humanity, the embittered Blake takes off. In space, Elaine appears and reveals her real identity—she was another android given to the grief-stricken senator when his real daughter committed suicide. Blake was duped into leaving, thinking there was nothing left for him on Earth, for he and Elaine are "really extensions of humanity, the hand and mind of mankind reaching out into the mysteries of all eternity." (Chapter 35)

The Werewolf Principle is obviously extrapolated from the many alien stories Simak had written earlier. Some of the best chapters in the book are those told from the various alien points of view of Thinker or Quester. Simak had an uncanny ability to step into the alien's shoes and describe alien feelings and thoughts. Again, Simak clearly affirmed his credo that among all races—human, alien, or android and Blake is all three—only intelligence has significance in the universe:

> Intelligence...is all there is; it's the one significance. Not life alone, not matter, not energy, but intelligence. Without intelligence, all this scattered matter, all the flaming energy, all the emptiness was of no consequence because it did not have a meaning. It was only intelligence that could take the matter and the energy and make it meaningful. (Chapter 35)

In this passage, Simak was enunciating a theme that he would devote whole novels to later, the use of intelligence to search for the first Principle behind the order of the universe.

3. THE GOBLIN RESERVATION

A case might be made that *The Werewolf Principle* is not too much different from the bulk of Simak's "sympathetic alien" stories, but with the publication of *The Goblin Reservation*, Simak really began writing those strange un-Simakian novels that distressed critics like P. Schuyler Miller so much.

As long as Simak treated his fantasy as humor, some reviewers did not seem to mind the presence of fantasy critters in a supposedly science-fiction novel—as long as they were presented as aliens sent to Earth eons ago. In *The Goblin Reservation*, Simak included them all—goblins, ghosts, trolls, banshees, ghosts, and even a dragon. For good measure, Simak also tossed in the pot a Neanderthal named Alley Oop working on his doctorate, Shakespeare's ghost and the Bard himself, a saber-tooth tiger named Sylvester, a *doppelgänger* college professor, and a mysterious artifact levitated right out of Clarke's *2001*. All of the action is set at a college in Wisconsin, and the protagonist is a professor of supernatural phenomena who has just returned from the stars (in the type of matter transmitter used in *Way Station*) to find that a duplicate of himself, returned before him, has been murdered. From this point on, the plot is a mixture of fantasy and comic opera as the professor tries to solve his own murder, unravel the mystery of the artifact, rescue a painter lost in time, and thwart some nasty aliens, all with the magical help of the assorted company of folklore aliens.

Simak always looked back fondly at *The Goblin Reservation* whenever any interviewer asked him about it, because "I had so much fun writing it." Simak had a reputation among science-fiction authors as a humorist, but he had mostly used humor to lightly season his works when things became too serious. Up until *The Goblin Reservation*, he had never consciously set out to write a purely humorous novel. He took light jabs at several hoary traditions—time travel, space opera, ancient astronauts who colonize Earth, and college administrations—and interpolated a terrific bar and brawl scene that George Lucas might have envied. The only "serious" passages are the wonderful descriptions of the autumn Wisconsin landscape—no science-fiction author had a better feel for the beauties of the outdoors than Simak.

4. *OUT OF THEIR MINDS*

Simak waited a year to write a new novel, but then he pulled out all the stops, continuing in the same uncharacteristic manner, in *Out of Their Minds* (1970). Lester del Rey tagged the novel "kitsch" and, after praising the suspense in the story, cried uncle at Simak for letting "myth-creation...run rampant. Goblins and werewolves were enough. But when we are asked to believe that men have believed in comic book characters and such for long enough and deeply enough to have turned them into myth creatures at least as real as the devil, we boggle a bit. And when the Civil War gets dragged in as a myth, it is too thick..."[7]

Brer Rabbit, Don Quixote, the Wicked Witch of the North, and the Devil himself are all characters in this novel about the adventures of Horton Smith, a television and radio newsman on his way home to Pilot Knob. In the very first chapter, his car gets run off the road by a dinosaur, and he is invited in for supper at a cabin inhabited by a man and woman who look surprisingly like the comic strip hillbillies Snuffy and Lowizie. Smith had read a manuscript by a history professor who advanced the theory that humanity's imagination has created a world of creatures from the "energy of thought" that will, in the course of evolution, supersede the human race. Three times someone or something has tried to kill him, and Smith realizes anyone who reads this manuscript is in terrible danger from these unseen forces.

Smith and his girl friend leave Pilot Knob and start out for Washington, DC, but are sidetracked into a delightful alternate world populated by characters from comic strips, folktales, and literature. They meet Mickey Mouse and Pluto, Don Quixote and Sancho Panza, and the Devil himself, who warns that the fantasy creatures have a plan, but the Devil won't reveal what it is.

Horton suddenly wakes up in the thick of the Battle of Gettysburg but fought just as Civil War buffs have imagined it. When one of Lovecraft's monsters from the Cthulhu mythos appears, Horton is snapped back into the "real" world, where he finds that all means of transportation and communication have been enchanted to a stop. The Devil appears at the White House and makes his quirky demands— more truly evil characters must be imagined, or the wheel or fire will be next to go. Smith saves the day by rendering the Devil helpless in an iron fence, and Sancho Panza tortures the Devil into reversing the spell by throwing water on him, remembering that imaginary creatures must play by the rules humans have imagined.

Like *The Goblin Reservation, Out of Their Minds* is great fun to read. The inventive scenes in which Horton Smith's life is threatened by sea serpents, werewolves, dinosaurs, and other assorted perils, natural and unnatural, keep the pages turning. Simak tacked on a stereotypical fantasy ending, traditional good triumphing over traditional evil, yet there is gentle irony in the Devil's plan to bring technological America to its knees by putting its automobiles and telephones under a spell. The novel can still qualify as science fiction, for Simak did attempt a rationale for his imaginary creatures, playing fast and loose with a philosophy of evolution. Simak had dabbled in earlier stories with imagined creatures becoming real with the help of electronics (see the discussion of "Shadow Show" above), but never on such a grand scale nor with the help of evolutionary pressures.[8]

5. DESTINY DOLL

In the last of this series of zany novels, *Destiny Doll* (1971), Simak was the victim of critical misunderstanding when he made a serious attempt to be more "literary." He told Thomas D. Clareson that he thought *Destiny Doll* was the first time he had ever tried to write a story on two different levels. Apparently critics were still reeling at his change of pace from works like *City* and *Way Station* to *The Goblin Reservation* and *Out of Their Minds*. The novel was "less than satisfactory," said the *Minneapolis Star*,[9] and P. Schuyler Miller again disgustedly condemned its mixture of science fiction and fantasy.[10]

Destiny Doll follows a favorite pattern of Simak's, the quest. A band of adventurers are marooned on a strange planet, outside a colossal white city. The company includes Captain Mike Ross, fugitive and planet hunter; Sara Foster, rich big-game huntress bankrolling the expedition; Friar Tuck, a phony religious; and George Smith, a blind man who leads them to the planet by receiving a telepathic signal. They have come in search of another earlier explorer who landed on the planet with a telepathic robot and mysteriously disappeared. Other ships have been similarly disabled as theirs, and they wonder what happened to all the other visitors.

The band is greeted by hobbies, robots in the form of hobby-horses, who warn them to get inside the city before darkness. In the city, they discover a "doorway" to other worlds, and they are all shanghaied to a desert planet where they find a strange but powerful alien called Hoot. By combining their mental powers as if in a *séance*, the five are transported back to the city.

The five companions traverse the planet, through desert and badlands and into the mountains, looking for other visitors. They encounter plenty of exotic and dangerous flora and fauna in this Land of Oz: orchards of huge trees who throw poison seeds at the company which are then collected by rat-like creatures (when Ross cuts down one of the trees, creatures resembling snails crawl out of the top, their sorrow at losing their home making the band feel terrible guilt); Centaurs with whose champion Ross fights a duel; and the terrible Raveners, monstrous flying carnivores. The band come upon a battlefield littered with piles of bones, grisly evidence of the Raveners' attack on the humans who brought the hobbies. Early in the quest, Tuck finds a crudely carved doll—in its face a heart-wrenching sadness and the "misery of existence"—for which he develops a Madonna-like obsession. The companions finally locate the explorer, trapped and completely happy in an "enchanted" valley resembling ancient Greece, with absolutely no desire to leave.

One by one, each of the humans, following his or her own "destiny," drops out: the blind man simply vanishes, Sara returns to the valley, and Tuck, leaving the doll, fades away. Hoot, after joining minds with Ross, reminiscent of the alien contacts in earlier novels like *Time and Again* and *Time Is the Simplest Thing*, metamorphoses into his "third self" and is gone. Only Ross and the explorer's telepathic robot, Roscoe, are left to return to the city, narrowly escaping the ugly Raveners.

Safe in the city, Ross tries to tie up all the loose ends and explain the company's disappearances. The trees were really "thought receivers" that stored the knowledge of the galaxy in seeds, but when will the alien orchard keepers who planted the trees come to reap the knowledge harvest? Simak used this idea of knowledge-gathering devices left by an alien race in some earlier short stories ("Jackpot" and "Junkyard," see above), but the biological method is a new wrinkle. Sara returns and Ross, in a mystical moment of epiphany (and just as they are about to be attacked by the Raveners), has the answer. The planet is a "many-layered reality," a jumping-off place from which the others were able to will themselves into alternate worlds, and the doll is the symbol of the shock of recognition that

There were many universes and many sentient levels and at certain time-space intervals they became apparent and each of them was real, as real as the many geologic levels that a geologist could count. Except that this was not a matter of counting: it was seeing and sensing and knowing they were there (Chapter 28).

Sara and Mike join the rest of the company. Not knowing how, but "filled with mystic faith," all took the step "out into the infinite unknowing" and found a familiar Simakian pastoral paradise, "a place that was everlasting and unchanging with room for everyone." It is this same kind of leap of faith that will start critics in the 1970s talking about the "mystic" Simak.

Destiny Doll is an appropriate culmination in this series of strange novels beginning with *The Werewolf Principle*. The company's quest to find the missing visitors is an the second refers to the ultimate purpose of the universe embodied in intelligent life.

Simak had faith in an orderly universe. He could not accept the concept that the orderliness of the universe was merely the result of chance, but believed there was a "Principle which guides the universe, an overseeing power or plan." Simak made no bones about the nature of this Principle—it, unlike the Judaeo-Christian God, may be uncaring or indifferent, but if it happens to be a caring, compassionate being, "we cannot be so provincial that we must insist God is for man alone and for this planet alone."[2]

Linked closely with his speculations on the nature of God embodied in the Principle was a desire to understand the purpose of life and, what was even more precious to Simak, the reason for intelligent life. Again, he could not accept life as purposeless, the accidental result of a random evolutionary process; rather, life itself could very well be the *raison d'être* of the universe and intelligence the highest expression of that purpose. What upset and saddened him was that humanity had too often used the gift of intelligence to understand physical laws "hung with dollar signs."[3] Simak ardently believed that "if the same efforts and the same funding had been expended to understand social, economic, and political concepts as have been used to build a better and more complex technology, we might now have not only a better life, but even now stand closer to the real purpose of intelligence, to bring about a complete understanding of the universe."[4]

Such metaphysical conjecturing in his fiction earned Simak the title of a "mystic" writer, which he respectfully declined. He modestly asserted that all he had done was to ask questions and to attempt to make some rather "quiet suggestions" on certain basic factors of human existence. These questions and speculations had been boiling around in his mind for years, yet he couldn't see how to write a story based on them. He attempted once in an earlier story, "The Spaceman's Van Gogh" (*Original Science Fiction Stories*, March 1956). An art critic teleports himself to a planet in search of information about an artist who died there. He finds evidence that the artist has brought Christian love to the planet's aborigines through his painting. Looking beyond its sentimentality, the story is more significant for its dialectic between the "faith" that gives humans the power to travel through space and the search for the scientific principle behind this power. In this story, Simak first mentioned the need for a quest to search out an Universal Principle greater than both faith and fact.

1. *A CHOICE OF GODS*

The end result of all this soul-searching was *A Choice of Gods* (1972), which Simak called his "final statement of values." Simak, needlessly worried that he would not have time to make another statement, claimed he wrote the novel to "get it off my neck."[5]

According to Simak, *A Choice of Gods* had "no hero, no villain, no structure, no drama, no violence, and no chase." P. Schuyler Miller called it "the strangest of the very strange books" Simak had been writing recently, although it was "closer to *City* in mood than anything else he has written."[6] The story begins in the year 2185 A.D. on an Earth deserted by humanity that in one night all teleported to the stars, except for a remnant of humans, including a small tribe of Indians, and the robots. No one knows exactly why the humans have departed so suddenly. The setting, much like *City*, is an Earth returning to a pristine wilderness in which the remaining humans, devoid of technological skills, are almost immortal because they are free of disease. The Indians have returned to their primitive ways, living off the land. Some of the robots continue to serve the humans, but other "wild robots" are building their own religiously-based society.

The story jumps ahead five-thousand years. Jason Whitney and his wife, like the Websters in *City*, have been living for five thousand years in the same house. They have remained alone, although they can readily communicate with the departed "People," including their many descendants scattered throughout the galaxy who flourish on innumerable planets and possess the power to travel freely throughout the universe. They receive a visit from their cousin from the center of the galaxy, who breaks the news that the People are on their way back to Earth. The humans have not been changed by their travels to the stars—they are brutal, arrogant, and materialistic in their use of technology—and will most certainly return to exploit Earth and destroy its Edenic way of life. Cousin John also brings news of the Principle, the central intelligence of the Galaxy, an aloof, uncaring intelligence, whose awareness of humanity may be likened to humanity's awareness of a microbe.

One of the Indian maidens, Evening Star, discovers that she can converse with the trees and animals of the woods and, more than any human, has an insight into the reality of the community of life throughout nature. She falls in love with another parapsychic, David, a "pilgrim" from the West and descendant of agricultural workers who is a "healer" with the power to kill or cure all creatures, even aliens. David "cures" the sorrow of an ugly alien resembling a can of worms, who came to Earth seeking his "soul." When David and Evening Star join their powers, they have a revelation of the wholeness and purpose of the universe.

Concerned about the return of the People, Jason and his Indian friend Red Cloud (despite Red Cloud's misgivings—Indians dislike and distrust all machines) reluctantly visit the wild robots. The robots have been busy perfecting the "Project," a super-robot who has taken command of their society and has achieved communication with the Principle, becoming its spokesman. But when the Project first contacts the Principle, it shows little interest, replying that "humanity is a transient factor and is none of our concern" (Chapter 22).

As Simak warned, the novel reaches no carefully planned resolution. When representatives of the People arrive, the robots give them the message, through the "Project," that Earth in its present condition is part of a deliberate experiment by the Principle, with which the People must not interfere.

Critics were dissatisfied with Simak's leaving human destiny in the hands of a cold, unknowable intelligence, yet praised the novel for its warmth and humanity, its similarity to *City* in its "subtle, but very intense exploration into the purpose of man's existence, his future, and his philoso-

phy"[7]—and its thorough-going pastoralism. Simak reiterated
this pastoralism in the survivors' fear of what the People will
do to the environment and the simple way of life exemplified
by the Indians. The Indians are not the Native Americans of
American history books, but a race which has absorbed the
better aspects of white culture and represent the ideal of
harmony with nature. As Jason tells Red Cloud, "Your people don't go to the stars. There may be no need of you to do
so. You have become, instead, a part of your environment,
living within its texture and understanding" (Chapter 3). As
Jenkins said of the dogs in *City*, the Indians and robots must
have the freedom to work out their own destinies without the
double "fatal disease" that still obsesses humanity, property
and profit. If the People return with their technology, the
"old profit motive and the subsidiary philosophies that depended on it" would be re-established, and Earth's future
would again be in the hands of a technological civilization
that is never satisfied, but "must expand or die" (Chapter 31).

Even the development of parapsychic powers is ham-
pered by technology, for the two seem to be mutually exclusive. David and Evening Star have experienced their psychic
leaps simply because of their closeness to nature and their
ignorance of scientific knowledge. David "cannot read and
does not know about the stars." Their union will extend their
oneness with nature into the universe and make their children
the next step on the evolutionary scale.

Simak took his usual swipe at organized Christianity
by having the robots take it up when humanity abandons it.
When asked, Simak was not very clear why he joined robots
to religion, other than "robots are submissive" and "he
thought it might be a good idea."[8] He later extended the
concept to a robot Pope who summons Vatican-17 in *Project
Pope* (1981). Jason Whitney reflects that religion was once
meaningful before it became "manifested in lordly buildings
filled with pomp and glitter rather than being nourished in
the human heart and mind." And now it was kept alive by
"beings that were not even human, machines that had been
accorded a measure of seeming humanness purely as a matter of technology and pride" (Chapter 5).

3. *OUR CHILDREN'S CHILDREN*

In 1974, Simak returned to a theme he could never resist writing about for very long—the alien encounter. A few years earlier, his novella, "The Thing in the Stone" (*Worlds of If*, March 1970), was a return to those sentimental stranded alien stories of the fifties and sixties. The protagonist, an old man, the typical Simak loner who sits in his rocking chair and walks the hills, can listen to the stars. He is conscious of a creature buried deep in the limestone floor of an old wildcat den. The old man is trapped in the cave but frees himself by going back in time millions of years when the alien is exiled. The story ends on a question: does the old man have the right to free the alien exile? To get an answer, he will ask the stars. Despite the fact that Simak has done this story over and over, the descriptions of the countryside and of the joys of living alone in the hills contain some of his best writing. The fans were still enamored with this type of story, for it won the 1970 Nebula runner-up for Best Novella and the 1971 Hugo Second Best Novella.

But for his 1974 novel, *Our Children's Children*, serialized in *Worlds of If* (June-August 1973), Simak chose the nasty alien encounter, only this time complicating the plot with time travel. At the astonishing rate of two million per hour, people from the peaceful Utopian future of 2498 A.D., five hundred years hence, are pouring through time tunnels and creating economic havoc. Hot in pursuit are bloodthirsty alien invaders who kill for the sake of killing, and the people of the future, without weapons technology, are doomed unless they flee to the Miocene period, twenty-five million years ago. They have stopped five-hundred years back to acquire the necessary technology and strongly suggest that the present population go back to avoid invasion.

In addition to the overcrowding problems caused by all these refugees from the future, the alien monsters start coming through the time tunnel. All are destroyed but one, but it must be found as soon as possible before it lays eggs. The monsters are multiplying (they have a fantastically accelerated evolutionary development), and the U.S. gov-

ernment must take the lead in securing international cooperation to build the time tunnels and in mobilizing an army to
destroy the aliens. The people of the future will trade the
secrets of fusion power and a cure for cancer in exchange for
time tunnels back to the past.

Largely through the efforts of the press, the crisis is
at last resolved, even with the cooperation of the Russians.
When threatened, the aliens instinctively disappear into the
past to the time of the dinosaurs (there are implications that
this may be the solution to the disappearance of the dinosaurs). Simak had used a variant of this idea in an earlier
short story, "Small Deer" (*Galaxy*, October 1965). In this
story, Simak made aliens responsible for the sudden disappearance of the dinosaurs—they were rounding them up and
slaughtering them for food—and as soon as our population
grows large enough to attract their attention, the aliens could
come back.

Our Children's Children was crafted well, the nasty
aliens were exciting, but the novel was not sufficiently different from other alien invasion stories except for the time
travel twist. It was ordinary, but not extraordinary Simak.

4. *THE ENCHANTED PILGRIMAGE*

Simak had always been sensitive to the demands of
the market, and when the fantasy boom came along in the
seventies, he was one of the first to climb on the bandwagon.
He had always considered himself a "soft science" writer and
had never been squeamish about stirring fantasy elements
into his plots when it suited him. It only seemed perfectly
natural that he should publish his first "pure" fantasy in 1975
and give it an appropriate fantasy quest title, *The Enchanted
Pilgrimage*. All the action takes place in a delightful medieval alternate universe, where magic really works. Simak
borrows Tolkien's recipe by mixing up goblins, gnomes,
hermits, furry halflings, brownies, elves, fairies, ogres, and
trolls. In addition, he adds a pinch of Lovecraft (the Chaos
Beast), sprinkles in characters very like those from the Oz
books (the Tin Bucket and Alexander Jones, a kind of Wizard of Oz on a trail bike who obviously comes from our

trees. A huge robot appears and explains that humanity did go to the stars and brought back some of the aliens the company met along the way. A small group of scientists and engineers established the Place as a library for knowledge gathered from other civilizations in the Galaxy, but the retrieval system is not working. With the help of the psychics, this knowledge could be tapped, technology rediscovered, and humans put back on the track. The story should end here, but Tom, like Natty Bumppo, goes into the nomad village and gets himself captured—then rescued in the nick of time by his grotesque buddies.

In the wake of his Nebula Grand Master Award granted the same year, Simak won the 1977 Jupiter Award offered by the Instructors of Higher Education for this novel. It would not do to chide college professors for their choice, but *Heritage* is a distinctly derivative novel, a replay of previous themes that Simak explored so well in 1972 in *A Choice of Gods*, with one glaring exception. The purpose of the quest is to restore technology to the human race, a complete change of heart for Simak who, since *City*, had regarded technology as the curse of humanity and had made it responsible for its failure as an intelligent race. Technology and psi powers in human society had been mutually exclusive in earlier novels, but here psi powers are the instrument of restoring technology to humankind. In its favor, however, the novel does have an appealing collection of Simakian aliens and robots to lighten up its more serious moments.

7. *MASTODONIA*

The chapter on the early Simak showed Simak's continuing fascination with time travel, especially travel back to the Pleistocene period when the great mammals dominated the Earth. In the seventies, Simak's interest in things prehistoric was rekindled, probably as the natural result of his research as feature science writer on the *Minneapolis Star*, for in addition to his fiction, he had written quite a number of articles and two books based on these subjects.[11] Almost all of his stories in the seventies had some element of time travel, and Simak rendered the time machine as obsolete as the spaceship. Using psi powers, his characters traveled billions of years back and forth in time just as easily as they invoked the same method to jump light years across the galaxy.

In the fifties and sixties, Simak had written a couple of short stories in which he imagined time travel employed by a business—profitably—to ferry tourists back in time. "Project Mastodon" (*Galaxy*, March 1955) had some entrepreneurial time travelers trying to form a separate nation in the past called Mastodonia. In "The Gleaners" (*Worlds of If*, March 1960), a corporation, in its avarice, attempts to violate the ethics of time travel—a foundation wants to send a traveler back to the Crucifixion when public opinion considers such a trip sacrilegious.

Simak resurrected the idea of traveling back to the Crucifixion as the subject of "The Marathon Photograph" (1974), one of three novellas anthologized by Robert Silverberg in *Threads of Time*. The story is told using the device of an unfinished manuscript. Two professors, one in geology and the other in Greek history, are vacationing in the Wisconsin hills. The geologist narrator is looking for a lost mine deserted by the miners because they found an object that started ticking each time they went into the cave "like it was trying to talk to them." The history professor finds a cube containing a holograph of the Battle of Marathon, evidence that someone from the future has traveled in time.

The plot rapidly thickens as the professors meet the time travelers from the future who are searching for the cause of the nuclear wars that destroyed most of their past history. The ticking comes from a cylinder that the time travelers explain is a space capsule sent by an alien race whose sun went nova. One of the time travelers, Angela, treats the geologist to a time trip by joining minds and also to a psychic sexual experience. The story ends with the history professor disappearing into the past, and the geologist finding two more cubes. One is a photo of the coronation of Charlemagne, and the other of a crucifixion—but the cross is not tall, the ankles are tied not nailed, and there is no placard, no crown of thorns, and no two companions. Here the manuscript ends.

111

Thomas D. Clareson remarked on Simak's rather harsh judgment of Christianity in this climactic scene: "Simak presents a crucifixion utterly devoid of the glory Church and Scripture assigned to the Crucifixion."[12] But then Simak was at least as hard on organized religion as he was on technology. Nuclear war has devastated the future, and the time travelers were seeking its causes. When the geologist travels into the future, he catches a glimpse of a bleak, dark landscape, and the historians are very unlikable characters, products of that same gloomy future.

"The Marathon Photograph" contains some of Simak's most stylistically advanced writing. What Cliff always did well—the nature scenes—are among some of his best as the professors go tramping through Simak's beloved country, the Wisconsin hills. And the joining of minds with the woman from the future was as close to an intimate sexual scene as Simak ever managed. Simak was very fond of this story and disappointed that the critics completely overlooked it.

Simak wrote another somewhat inconsequential time travel story in 1974, "The Birch Clump Cylinder," for Judy-Lynn del Rey's first volume in an anthology series, *Stellar #1*. This story, also included by Lester del Rey in his *Best* anthology for 1975, is interesting primarily because it shows Simak's continuing preoccupation with the nature of time and its possible uses, an interest he never failed to mention in the many interviews he gave during the seventies. The "cylinder" is an engine using time as a source of energy which falls from an alien ship near a think tank. Graduates of the think tank are summoned back to find out how to turn off the time machine. One of the volunteers turns the control clockwise and disappears back into time; the other volunteer, the narrator, turns the control in the opposite direction and vanishes into the future. By then the device has been duplicated and used to send ships to the stars.

These earlier stories are preludes to his 1978 novel, *Mastodonia* (called *Catface* in Britain). A cat-faced alien lands on a retired college professor's property and litters it with time tunnels. A mastodon blunders through, and the college professor and his practical-minded girl friend get the idea to form Time Associates, a time travel company. They also proclaim the new nation of Mastodonia to beat the IRS and establish residence in the past. When the company organizes its first safari, their troubles begin. The fledgling company must fight off politicians (who want to relieve the population problem by sending unfortunates into the past), the State Department, and the churches who, of course, want to travel to the early Christian era. After State puts a ban on time travel, riots break out, and Mastodonia is recognized as an independent state. When the alien leaves, he grants the professor the power to engineer other time roads.

Mastodonia is pleasantly and warmly familiar, engendering *déjà-vu* as many elements from previous stories reappear: the small-town hero from Wisconsin accompanied by his dog; his friend, the village simpleton; the alien Catface from galactic headquarters who seems to be on assignment from the Principle; and businessmen and politicians who want to control the rights to time travel for their own interests. Except for the stronger love interest and the time travel business, this novel is *The Big Front Yard* slightly updated for the seventies.

8. *THE FELLOWSHIP OF THE TALISMAN*

Simak finished out the decade with two novels, which, like *Mastodonia*, are clearly derivative of previous offerings. In 1978, he wrote another medieval quest fantasy, *The Fellowship of the Talisman*, almost a sequel to *The Enchanted Pilgrimage*. The setting is medieval England in an alternate universe in which the world has remained in the Middle Ages for a thousand years, its progress thwarted by the evil influence of the Harriers.

The hero, Duncan Standish, must deliver a manuscript, historical proof of Jesus's existence, to Oxenford University for authentication. Duncan, reluctant to go but a dutiful son, is soon joined by that heterogeneous crowd that always accompanies Simak's fantasy heroes: a seven-foot giant, a huge killer mastiff, a war-horse, a gray burro, a bashful ghost, a hermit, a goblin, an old witch, a banshee, and the lady Diane mounted on a griffin. Harried by the Harriers,

113

who are aliens from the stars, the company stumbles onto an enchanted castle, where they meet a dotty wizard and an unfrocked demon named Scratch. (Simak always slipped in at least one memorable character, and Scratch is unforgettable.) The story ends in the inevitable confrontation between the company and the Harriers, who are really after the manuscript. The story, though sheer entertainment, is better constructed than *The Enchanted Pilgrimage* and proves that Simak could write entertaining commercial fantasy.

9. *THE VISITORS*

In 1979 Simak returned to writing for the magazines, and his new alien visitation novel, *The Visitors*, was serialized in *Analog* (October-December 1979). There is nothing really thematically new about *The Visitors*. It repeats ideas from earlier novels like *Ring Around the Sun* and shows some strong influences from the film *Close Encounters of the Third Kind*. A mysterious black box lands in Minnesota, and when an excited barber takes a potshot at the box, he is burned to a crisp. Along with other forms of life, a graduate student on a fishing trip is taken inside the box. The student receives a strong impression of home and that the box is somehow akin to a tree, but then the box disgorges him. News of a new satellite, which may be the mother ship, alerts the White House. Meanwhile, the visitor starts chewing up trees and spewing out bales of cellulose behind it. A shuttle confirms that the new satellite is a huge cluster of visitors waiting to come down to Earth. The government is uncertain what to do, when suddenly the visitor begins budding "babies" who start gulping down the cellulose. The visitor takes off, leaving its offspring behind.

Other visitors start landing everywhere in forests and lumberyards, but no one is actually harmed. The President chooses to sit tight and wait, despite pressures from religious cults, conservationists, and the military who covet the visitors' defense system. Just as suddenly as they came, the visitors begin leaving. In exchange for the trees, the visitors are budding biological "cars" that operate without fuel, fly through the air, and never crash. Another group is experimenting with making houses. The free cars and houses are causing economic panic, and this crisis forces international cooperation and a new economic world order. The story ends on an uneasy note—are the visitors making people, too?

The Visitors is a friendly alien story, the same kind of story that Simak wrote frequently in the fifties and sixties. All the visitors want is a source of cellulose and will barter with what they see is important to our technological society, automobiles and houses. The resulting economic dislocation forces an unexpected world peace and a world economic union to deal with the problem. As a Minnesotan where prejudice is rampant against the Native Americans, Simak made a strong appeal for their rights. He compared the "invasion" of the visitors to the invasion of the Native American by the white man and wondered—will the visitors take what they want without asking, ignoring human rights and behaving like arrogant, self-satisfied white men did with the Native Americans? Later, he drew another analogy to the "gift" of the visitors and our "gift" to the Native Americans; the Native Americans lost out because their technology was upset by the white man, when they wanted iron hatchets to replace their stone tomahawks. Ironically, the visitors had no sense that they had done anything wrong, that they had been in any way unjust. After all, they only consumed a few trees and left a piece of technology behind worth billions, ignorant of the economic consequences.

10. THE SHORT STORIES OF THE SEVENTIES

Simak had little time for writing short stories in the seventies, but of the few (only twelve) that he did write, he proved that he had not lost the skills he had carefully honed during the fifties and sixties. At least one of these stories qualified for the "mystic" label, "The Autumn Land" (*SF: Author's Choice 1971*), which was nominated for a Hugo in 1972 and came in third best. Simak used the flashback technique to tell the story of an out-of-work engineer who has a vision of nuclear catastrophe. The engineer steps through a "thinness" to a magic place where it is always autumn and time stands still. The needs of the few inhabitants are supplied by the Milkman, who explains that the autumn land is a halfway house where people can stop out, let their brains catch up, and sit in their rocking chairs until they are ready to go on.

In "Auk House" (*Stellar #3*, 1977), Simak resurrected the greedy corporation, this time practicing exploitation on a multi-dimensional level. An artist is sent through a rift of time to the age of the dinosaurs. He and other social misfits have been shanghaied to alternate worlds by the bosses of the prime world's "managed society." The alternate worlds are being exploited by big business interests from the prime world. A race of intelligent dinosaurs assures the artist that they will get rid of the invaders and protect the other alternate worlds from a similar fate.

"Construction Shack" (*Worlds of If*, February 1973) was also nominated for a Hugo and placed third. It is a nostalgic piece, a throwback to the type of work Simak did in the forties. A manned expedition to Pluto discovers that the planet is an artificial world, made of steel, a "construction shack" for "cosmic engineers" who "built" the solar system. In the opinion of the humans, they bungled the job, only creating one life-supporting world. So much for gods and their works...

Simak continued to write about humans with parapsychic powers, especially those who can travel to the stars without the aid of spaceships or those who can telepathically "listen to the stars." "Brother" (*The Magazine of Fantasy & Science Fiction*, October 1977) is the tale of a nature writer and his spaceman "brother." But there is no brother—the spaceman is a *doppelgänger* projection of the writer. "Party Line" (*Destinies*, November-December 1978) describes a government project of telepaths ranging the universe to communicate with alien intelligences for mutual benefits. The story ends in speculation about the listeners—have they evolved beyond humanity?

Most of the other stories that Simak wrote during this period end on this conjectural note. Simak also took time out to write one of his rare collaborations with his son Richard, "Unsilent Spring" (*Stellar #2*, 1976). Despite some flashes of Simakian humor, the story, based on the idea that the human body could adapt to DDT, exemplified Simak's filial devotion more than his writing skills.

It is easy to conclude that Simak was repeating himself thematically in the seventies. This was probably inevitable since he was turning out a novel, sometimes two, each year after his retirement from the newspaper in 1976. He was also solidifying his "mystic" philosophy about the nature of the universe, a philosophy that would help him shape a more consistent future history much different than what he had visualized in the fifties and sixties. He had extended the brotherhood of intelligent races to include the human race, and other intelligent races had taken on the task, in this projection of human history, of saving the human race from itself.

Always sensitive to what was selling, Simak had also turned to writing fantasy in the Tolkien mold, and, like Tolkien, inserting his unique brand of humor to leaven these serious confrontations between good and evil. One of Tolkien's strengths was always the comfortable and cheerful atmosphere of his company of questers and the sharp contrast in mood when they meet up with the forces of evil. Simak was able to capture that aspect of Tolkien's writing very successfully. He had adopted the quest as his pattern for most of his science-fiction novels, and his fantasy easily adapted to this model.

Although Simak's popularity fluctuated considerably—he was thirteenth in 1971, eighth in 1973, and plummeted to twenty-second in 1976—Simak's influence on the field and on younger writers was unmistakable. His colleagues rewarded his lifetime contributions to the field by making him Grand Master at the 1977 meeting of the Science Fiction Writers of America. In addition, he was Guest of Honor at Noreascon, the 29th World Science Fiction Convention. As his career moved into the 1980s and as he approached his eightieth year, he was not merely content to sit and rock but continued to produce creditable fiction almost until the day he died.

VII.

SIMAK'S LAST YEARS

1. *PROJECT POPE*

In the eighties Simak continued to be haunted by the same theme he thought might be his "final statement" in the early seventies, the search for the Principle, the key to the universe. He assigned this search to robots instead of humans in *Project Pope* (1981). For the last thousand years, a society of religious robots and humans has formed Vatican-17, a colony located on a planet, fittingly named End-of-Nothing, at the rim of the galaxy. This bizarre group has been engaged in a secret project, the ultimate infallible Pope, a computer Pope containing all the accumulated knowledge that can be gathered from the universe. Some of the Pope's input comes from psychic humans called Listeners who can travel mentally to other planets and record their experiences on "knowledge cubes" eventually fed into the Pope. Based on the Pope's knowledge rather than faith, the robots hope to establish a truly universal religion.

When one of the Listeners (appropriately called Mary) claims to have found Heaven, a religious crisis is precipitated. The "theological" faction of robots wants to have Mary canonized a saint, but Vatican-17 fears an end to the project if there is a fanatical resurgence of faith caused by Mary's "revelation." Into this situation comes Doctor Jason Tennyson, whose skills are desperately needed by Vatican-17 when the local physician dies, and Jill Roberts, a reporter who wants to write a formal history of the colony but is forbidden publication. Tennyson meets a former spaceman, Thomas Decker, who crash-landed on End-of-Nothing and now lives with an unseen companion, a collection of sparkling dust named Whisperer.

Decker thinks he might know where Heaven is—just before he took the lifeboat to End-of-Nothing, his ship was headed to a place similar to what Mary described. On Mary's second trip to Heaven, she is thrown out, the first time a Listener has ever encountered a direct reaction from one of the worlds.

Tennyson and Whisperer join minds and teleport to a strange world peopled by aliens who resemble mathematical equations. While Tennyson is gone, Decker is murdered by one of the robots. Concerned about the program, the Pope seeks advice from the humans. Jill and Tennyson learn the location of Heaven from the equation people and, with Whisperer's help, arrive on the planet. They meet a triad of aliens consisting of a "haystack" with thirteen eyes, a bubble named Smoky, and an octopus-like creature in constant motion nicknamed Plopper. To their surprise, the "murdered" Decker is alive—or rather his double—the original had been sent to End-of-Nothing. Founded by the Bubblies, Heaven turns out to be a Center of Galactic Studies, embarked on the same purpose as Vatican-17, but, unlike the Listeners at Vatican, Heaven collects its data physically, possessing the technology to recreate any life-form or artifact. The Bubbly Smoky is power-mad—his secret weapon is Plopper, a kind of living atomic bomb. Tennyson and the others must get back to Vatican with proof of Heaven's real nature.

Just as Plopper explodes, Whisperer abruptly transports them all back to End-of-Nothing, including the aliens. Heaven's real purpose is explained to the robot cardinal, and Vatican's search for the truth using the Listeners is restored.

The strengths of this novel lie in its carefully conceived aliens and in its concept of robots and humans bonding in a religious community to seek out ultimate truth. Its weakness is in the lack of drama in the resolution of the problems created in the novel. Heaven, for all of its alien wackiness, turns out to be rather dull, a data processing center as unexciting as the computer pope. In all these later novels, a center of galactic studies became Simak's standard ethical response to any crisis in human advancement, almost a reprise of earlier novels like *Way Station* where the cooperation of intelligent races was invoked to insure human and alien survival.

Ironically, the aliens, not the humans, become corrupted by their accumulated knowledge, a warning to the robots and humans that knowledge can also be power. Simak also cautioned against an excess of religious faith (engendered by Mary's so-called religious experience) standing in the way of a search for truth.

2. SPECIAL DELIVERANCE

In his next novel, *Special Deliverance* (1982), Simak continued with the concept of a Center for Galactic Studies. College professor Edward Lansing receives explicit instructions from a slot machine that translates him to an alternate world. He stumbles into an inn where he sees four men with skull-like faces playing cards and meets a company of puzzled pilgrims like himself: a jingoistic brigadier, a fanatic fundamentalist parson, a robot named Jurgens transplanted right out of *City*, a certified poetess, and a female engineer. All are from different worlds and different cultures and have no idea why they have been trapped on this world.

The company sets out for an unknown destination, and after a number of trials, each member of the quest disappears one by one, except for engineer Mary and Lansing. Some of the assorted dangers are familiar from other Simak novels; the company stops at a deserted city where the Brigadier and the Parson disappear through "portals" to other worlds, a device used in *Destiny Doll*. Lansing and Mary reenter a huge blue cube (its force-field had formerly rejected them) and find the four card-players.

The card-players are aliens from the far side of the galaxy, "social workers" conducting a search for qualified humans. The human race is threatened with extinction, obviously by its own stupidity (an old Simakian lament), and is at one of the "crisis points" of its evolutionary process. Humans from various alternate worlds have been recruited to this world to be subjected to a "test quest." (Earlier, Lansing and his sociologist colleague discuss the possibility that historic crisis points could be responsible for the existence of these alternate worlds.) Lansing and Mary have passed the test with flying colors and will be translated to a university where they will study how to become more fully human and join thousands of other humans in forming a new society.

Special Deliverance deals essentially with the same ideas as *Project Pope*, a place where galactic cooperation can be applied to the problems of the human race. Despite its similar theme and some interesting characters, *Special Deliverance* lacks the intellectual excitement of *Project Pope*. The evolution of humanity has reached an impasse and its only hope lies in some interference from other intelligent races. The aliens "test" humans for admittance to a galactic university, where they will get a second chance to preserve their intelligence as a survival factor. Aliens educating humans was not exactly a new idea with Simak—he introduced it as early as 1953 in his short story, "Kindergarten" (see Chapter VI above).

Contrarily, in *Project Pope* humans and robots are evolving without alien aid, seeking a higher "solution" through a marriage of the ideals of both science and religion, using human psychic powers to gather data by "listening to the stars." In both novels Simak was much more optimistic about the human race's ability to overcome the failure of its intelligence to help understand the purpose of life—a big departure from his earlier pessimism about human potential.

3. WHERE THE EVIL DWELLS

Simak balanced off such weighty matters with his third fantasy novel, *Where the Evil Dwells*, also published in 1982. The setting is a medieval alternate Earth where the Pax Romana has existed for two thousand years but is at last declining. The Roman legions have never succumbed to the barbarian hordes who are kept at bay by the "Evil," creatures dwelling in a buffer zone dangerous to humans called the Empty Land. The Evil are Simak's customary conglomerate of non-humans: unicorns, dragons, ogres, harpies, trolls, ghouls, goblins, banshees, and some nasty elementals—

121

things of evil spawned from dead and decaying matter similar to Theodore Sturgeon's "It."

A company of humans—Harcourt, a young lord grieving for his lost love Eloise captured by the Evil in a terror raid; Guy, the local abbot; and a housemaid Yolanda, who also happens to be a crack archer and expert woodcarver—and a Neanderthal called the Knurly Man, Harcourt's mentor, venture into the Empty Land. Harcourt is seeking Eloise and the abbot has news from Harcourt's dying uncle of a holy relic, a prism in which the soul of a saint has been imprisoned by a sorcerer.

On the way, the questers are joined by Simak's usual odd assortment of characters: a disgraced Roman centurion who fled the scene of a battle, an outcast troll in search of a bridge, a noble lady turned witch to study magic who also turns out to be Yolanda's grandmother, a wizard posing as a peddler, a parrot, and four wooden gargoyles who descend from a cathedral to help the company out of a tight spot.

Despite repeated attacks by the hordes of the Evil, the company fights its way to a Roman villa where the objects of the quest are housed. Ironically, the quest is a failure. Harcourt rejects Eloise who has become a pawn of the Evil, and the prism is dropped and shattered, releasing the spirit of the saint.

Yolanda marries Harcourt and everyone lives more or less happily ever after, except for the Knurly Man who gives his life to accomplish the quest. Somehow, *Where the Evil Dwells* does not satisfy like Simak's first two fantasies. Simak purified this fantasy of science-fiction elements, and the Evil are just folklore creatures, not aliens from the stars as in his previous fantasies. The quest is only mildly exciting, and even the humor seems forced. It is mainly provided by the bickering between the abbot and the Knurly Man who condemns religion as superstitious mumbo-jumbo and by such scenes as the troll without a bridge who bungles his own suicide.

4. THE SHORT STORIES OF THE EIGHTIES

Despite the fact that in the eighties Simak's novelistic powers were declining and his work was becoming too repetitious of earlier themes, he had not completely lost his touch for writing poignant, prize-winning short stories. In 1981 he won both the Hugo and the Nebula for Best Short Story for "Grotto of the Dancing Deer" (*Analog*, April 1980). Along with Catherine L. Moore, he was Guest of Honor at the 1981 Denvention to receive the award, the oldest writer ever to win a Hugo. "Grotto" is the kind of sentimental story that Simak does so well. A paleontologist working in the Pyrenees uncovers incontrovertible evidence that Luis, his assistant at camp, is a Cro-Magnon who has survived, impossible as it may seem, for 22,000 years. The heart of the story is the price that Luis has paid for his immortality, his solitude. Luis is the loneliest man in the world.

Simak wrote one other short story in the eighties, "The Whistling Well" (1980), for Kirby McCauley's anthology of original supernatural stories, *Dark Forces*. The story has a Lovecraftian flavor—a writer, investigating his genealogy, returns to his ancestral New England dwelling shunned by the local residents because of a well which makes whistling sounds. He sees loathsome shapes near the well which turn out to be intelligent dinosaurs who remind him that he is their "brother." Simak managed to work in two of his favorite science-fiction themes into what is supposedly a horror tale, dinosaurs with intelligence and the brotherhood of intelligent life.

5. *HIGHWAY OF ETERNITY*

Simak stopped writing anything new after 1982, and only a few close friends knew that he was ill with leukemia and emphysema. In a letter I received in September 1985, Simak reluctantly explained that he was slowly recovering from his own illness and also that his wife Kay had suffered a stroke in September of 1984 and was now in a rest home. Under these difficult circumstances, he had suspended all writing projects for the last three years, but now he had started to write again, making a fair start on a short story. The short story never did see publication, but in June of 1986, at the age of eighty-two, Simak was back with what turned out to be his last novel, *Highway of Eternity*. *Highway of Eternity* is, as fittingly described on the dust jacket, a *tour-de-force*, probably one of the most convoluted novels Simak, or anyone else, ever wrote. The plot twists and turns all over time and space and repeats many of the ideas about the future of the human race that had been pestering Simak since he wrote *A Choice of Gods* in 1972.

Jay Corcoran has summoned his friend, Tom Boone, who has an uncanny ability "to step around corners," to investigate a room-sized box stuck somehow to the outside of a hotel suite occupied by one of Corcoran's clients, Martin, who mysteriously vanished. Corcoran also has a talent, an ability to visualize what ordinary people cannot see, which has made him wealthy. In the pressure of the moment—the hotel is being torn down while they are investigating the room—Boone does "step around a corner" into the box, taking Corcoran with him.

The box turns out to be a traveler, a machine that can traverse time and space. Boone and Corcoran are transported instantly back to a time bubble in 1745 in Shropshire, England, where they meet a strange family of refugees— from a million years in the future. The family has fled to the past to escape the Infinites, intelligences from the galactic center who are busy converting corporeal humans into incorporeal entities, part of a plan by the Infinites to preserve a corpus of intelligence from all races. Timothy, the scholar of the family, has been studying human history to find out where the race went wrong, a familiar Simakian dirge. A brother, Henry, has been converted into a ghost—he was rejected by the Infinites halfway through his conversion. Henry is a scout for the group, for he can travel in space and time outside the bubble without a traveler. The rest of the family consists of David, who does not do much but tramp around the estate with a playful alien nicknamed Spike; his beautiful sister Enid, the "thinker" who prophesies that trees will succeed man; and his older sister and brother-in-law,

124

Emma and Horace. Corcoran's missing client turns out to be their twentieth-century contact, Martin, whom David distrusts.

The refugees are scattered by the appearance of a "monster," a robot assassin in the form of a spider web twelve feet across pulsing with dangerous energy. Unable to operate the traveler, Enid and Boone end up in southwestern North America of 50,000 B.C. When the monster catches up with them, Enid is able to escape in the traveler, but Boone remains. An angry bison shatters the monster except for its braincase. Befriended by a wolf, Boone sets out to find water. He has been dreaming of a figure with a hat, who speaks to him about the "brotherhood of life." Boone catches his leg in a crevice and cannot free himself. Simak loved to write about this prehistoric time period, and this section contains some of the best writing in the novel—especially the descriptions of the landscape and the animals and the gripping action scenes.

Meanwhile, Enid lands on a planet where she meets Horseface, an alien with whom she melds minds to construct a net that can travel anywhere in time and space. Suddenly, Horseface and Enid are translated to a Disneyworld planet with purple grass and pink trees. Enid scares off some aliens having a picnic and picks up what looks like a television set but with extraordinary powers—whatever anyone thinks appears on the screen. Horseface returns, carrying a chest, pursued by a purple alien with tentacles. They narrowly escape the alien on the net, but just before they do, Enid sees Boone on the television screen.

Corcoran and David travel forward to 975,000 A.D., a future Simak frequently predicted with robots caring for humans in a pastoral Utopia where all humans have to do is sit around, think, and philosophize, "a horrible way for the human race to end" (Chapter 8). Corcoran has one of his "visions," a colossal tree stretching up to the sky, with a staircase winding around its trunk. Henry returns, telling them where Boone is but that Enid has disappeared. They go back to find Boone, but he, too, is gone. Horribly, David is attacked and devoured by a saber tooth cat. The braincase of the monster pleads with Corcoran to take it with him, but he refuses.

Boone finally frees himself by "stepping around a corner" and takes Wolf with him. He finds himself on a dull gray planet, where he sees a trolley track. Boone and Wolf hop on a car that halts at a building with tables and chairs, where they are served by a robot chef. (Simak's characters always seem to eat well on their quests, even among bizarre surroundings.) At one of the tables is the Hat, who explains that they are on the Highway of Eternity, and then collapses into a bundle of clothes. Enid and Horseface appear and everybody exchanges adventures.

Horseface opens the chest, and a doughy mass flows out, forming a huge map of the galaxy, several miles in diameter and in its center runs a white line, representing a highway among the stars. They enter the map and spot a yellow star with a precise X on it.

The rest of the family—Timothy, Horace, Emma, and the alien Spike—land fifty-thousand years beyond the time they fled in the past near one of the monasteries built by the Infinites. All that is left of the human race is a sparkling and twinkling on the hills. They meet some wild robots and see a killer monster, but Spike drives it off. With the robots for protection, they enter the monastery, and while Spike and the monster are engaged in combat, the entire company is translated to another planet. They travel for days, and come upon a junkyard. The monster attacks Timothy, but Spike sends it over a cliff. A flier picks up Timothy and takes him to a city that turns out to be a Galactic Center, where thinkers and investigators from all over the galaxy pool theories and discoveries. Spike recruited the family for the Center—he is a talent scout who also hunts down killer robots. The panel at Galactic Central informs Timothy that the Infinites have been quarantined on their planet for their arrogance, and their Enforcers, the killer robots, have been hunted down.

Events begin to happen with a confusing suddenness worthy of A. E. van Vogt. Corcoran has returned to the place where he saw the tree. He now sees the tree and begins climbing. About four miles up, he falls and is precipitated into the Highway land. He boards the trolley, meets up with Boone, Enid, and Horseface, and breaks the tragic news of David's death. Enid's traveler appears, with Martin and three Infinites, who claim to be refugees themselves. The Hat returns, suggesting a new destination, the Rainbow People, and they all leave on the net, except for Martin. They land on a crystal planet where the Hat tells them the Infinites will be judged for their wreckage of the human race by the Rainbow People, the most ancient race in the Universe. After the Rainbow People render judgment, Boone, Enid, and Wolf are suddenly translated to another planet where Enid is battered with a "wind" of information—"my mind is full to bursting" (Chapter 14). Then Horseface and the net pick them up, and they travel to the planet marked with an X on the map.

Meanwhile, Henry, lonely and depressed without his family, travels to the end of the world, a bloated red sun reminiscent of Wells's *The Time Machine*. The trees have inherited the Earth but are not aware of their dominance. Henry talks to one of the trees, and although it can think and talk, the tree is senile and forgetful, another failure of evolution.

The star with the X is, of course, the Galactic Center where the family is reunited except for Henry. Corcoran will return to the twentieth century, and Boone will stay with Enid. Martin was dumped on Earth in the twenty-third century without a traveler, where the world is in a state of economic collapse, reverting to an agrarian life-style very similar to the Earth in *City*. Martin stumbles on the braincase of the killer robot and uses it to start a new religion that preaches finding one's true self and rejecting technology and materialistic progress, the attitude that eventually undermined the human race. At the Center, Timothy unearthed a copy of a document that mentions the formation of just such a religion founded on a "mysterious artifact."

All the crazy events and coincidences are the plans of the aliens Horseface and the Hat. Horseface, the last surviving member of his race, is a busybody who must meddle in the lives of other races, trying to help them develop their intelligence to their fullest capacities. He had preserved the family by letting them think they stole the secret of time

127

travel from the Infinites. He manipulated events so that Boone would meet the family, for Boone's ability is the answer to the problems of the human race, an entirely new psychic talent. Perhaps the union of Enid and Boone will produce a new and tougher race, another giant step in human evolution. All the loose ends are tied up—except for returning Henry to the family and leaving the Hat to keep an eye on them.

Despite the complexities of the plot, Simak is back on very familiar ground. The human race, again by its own disastrous decisions, is about to disappear, and aliens, following the code of preserving intelligence as a duty of all intelligent races, must step in and rearrange events before a final catastrophe can occur. Horseface sets up the moves on the chessboard, and the humans, following the good side of their natures, travel the squares. Simak, in his last three novels, seemed to be saying that the humans willing to preserve the last vestiges of their own human nature are the only ones worth saving, but they cannot do it without help. Rather than have the human race disappear and be replaced by another more worthy intelligence as he did in *City*, Simak called on the brotherhood of intelligence to save humanity. And, in this final novel, he completely reversed his previous stand that technology was a danger to human survival—the humans who reject technology to live in a pastoral paradise eventually become the victims of the Infinites.

Highway of Eternity was Simak's swan song to a long and rich career as a science-fiction writer. It is fitting that, in the twilight of his life, a writer, who long warned us of the dangers of the misuse of our intelligence, also gave us a scenario full of promise and hope—that life should be lived in the company of other intelligent beings. It may take us another million years to realize it, but our essential humanity is safe.

VIII.

CONCLUSION:
SIMAK FOR THE FUTURE

It is appalling that Clifford D. Simak seems to be slipping into publishing oblivion. Other Golden Age writers (as many seem to think of Simak today) such as Heinlein and Asimov remain in print, while Simak's books are becoming increasingly difficult to find. Even *City*, which had been continuously in print for forty years, went out of print from 1988 to 1992, when it was reissued in paperback by Macmillan Collier. But even worse is the lack of critical attention being paid to a Grand Master. Only a handful of articles have even mentioned Simak; perhaps this full-length study of Simak will revive at least some critical interest in a writer who has influenced so many other science-fiction writers, not the least of which was the prolific Dr. Asimov. As an appendix, I have included a list of recent reprints of Simak's work right up to the time of the publication of this book, and I hope that the science-fiction world will make an effort to repay this Grand Old Man a debt by bringing him back into print.

NOTES

PREFACE

[1]Roald D. Tweet, "Clifford D. Simak: 1904- ," *Science Fiction Writers: Critical Studies of the Major Authors from the Early Nineteenth Century to the Present Day*, ed. E. F. Bleiler (New York: Scribner's, 1982): 517.

CHAPTER I

[1]Kingsley Amis, *New Maps of Hell: A Survey of Science Fiction* (New York: Harcourt, Brace, 1960), 74.
[2]Biographical data on Simak has been gleaned from the chapter on Simak in Sam Moskowitz, *Seekers of Tomorrow: Masters of Modern Science Fiction* (Cleveland: World, 1965); Muriel Becker's superb bibliography (see note 3 below); a taped interview with Simak conducted by Thomas D. Clareson; and reluctantly—from the author himself. Simak read the draft of this chapter and noted any slight discrepancies reported in other sources.
[3]Muriel Becker, *Clifford D. Simak: A Primary and Secondary Bibliography* (Boston: G. K. Hall, 1980), xiv.
[4]"Where's Hawk Carse?" *Ad Astra*, July 1939: 2-5.
[5]Thomas D. Clareson, "Clifford D. Simak: The Inhabited Universe," *Voices for the Future: Essays on Major Science Fiction Writers*, ed. Thomas D. Clareson (Bowling Green: Bowling Green University Popular Press, 1976), 1:75.
[6]Algis Budrys, "Galaxy Bookshelf," *Galaxy*, July-August 1971: 162.
[7]Becker, xxiv-xxv.
[8]David Pringle, "Aliens for Neighbours: A Reassessment of Clifford D. Simak," *Foundation: The Review of Science Fiction*, March 1977: 17.

[9]Paul Walker, *Speaking of Science Fiction* (Oradell, NJ: Luna Publications, 1978), 58.
[10]Algis Budrys, "Books," *The Magazine of Fantasy & Science Fiction*, September 1982: 26.

CHAPTER II

[1]Isaac Asimov, ed. *Before the Golden Age: A Science Fiction Anthology of the 1930's* (Garden City, NY: Doubleday, 1974), 180.
[2]Sam Moskowitz, "Religion in Science Fiction: God, Space, and Earth," *Amazing*, April 1965: 94-95.
[3]"The Creator" was reprinted as a chapbook by Locus Press in 1981 in commemoration of Simak's fiftieth anniversary as a writer.
[4]Walker, 63.
[5]Isaac Asimov, *In Memory Yet Green: The Autobiography of Isaac Asimov, 1920-1954* (New York: Avon Books, 1980), 213.
[6]Pringle, 16.

CHAPTER III

[1]Clareson, 75.
[2]The dedication of *City* is to Simak's beloved Scottish terrier, Scootie, who *is* Nathaniel.
[3]Jason Pascoe, "Clifford Simak: The Compassionate Universe." *Winding Numbers*, No. 2 (Summer): 22-23.

CHAPTER IV

[1]See notes on the Clareson and Pringle essays at the end of Chapter I above.
[2]Clareson, 75.
[3]Brian Aldiss, *The Billion Year Spree: The True History of Science Fiction* (Garden City, NY: Doubleday, 1973): 235.
[4]*Empire* may be counted as a novel, even though it is a Campbell rewrite and a forgettable historical curiosity.

[5]An alien plant paid a similar visit in an earlier story, "Green Thumb," *Galaxy*, July 1954, and was cared for by the county agricultural agent until the alien's companions returned for him.

[6]In "Small Deer," *Galaxy*, October 1965, Simak tells the story about a time traveler who goes back and discovers aliens herding up dinosaurs for food, which accounts for the dinosaurs' sudden disappearance as a species. The ending of the story chillingly implies that our human population might have grown enough for the aliens to consider coming back.

[7]See Chapter I above.

[8]Except for Campbell's *Empire*, Simak never collaborated with anyone again until 1977, when he and his son, Richard Simak, wrote "Unsilent Spring."

[9]P. Schuyler Miller, "The Reference Library," *Analog*, April 1964: 93.

[10]*From Atoms to Infinity: Readings in Modern Science* (New York: Harper & Row, 1965).

CHAPTER V

[1]These figures all come from Mike Ashley's *The Illustrated Book of Science Fiction Lists* (New York: Simon & Schuster, 1982), 19.

[2]Becker, xxv.

[3]All these quotes from Simak taken from Walker, 58.

[4]Simak only wrote one "pure" horror story, "The Questing of Foster Adams" (*Fantastic Universe*, August-September 1953), a *Weird Tales* yarn in which a recluse historian sells his soul to the Devil in exchange for authentic historical details.

[5]Algis Budrys, "Galaxy Bookshelf," *Galaxy*, June 1967: 191-192.

[6]Judith Merril, "Books," *The Magazine of Fantasy & Science Fiction*, May 1967: 46-48.

[7]Lester del Rey, "Reading Room," *Worlds of If*, July-August 1970: 148:149.

[8]In "Worrywart," *Galaxy*, September 1953, an invalid has the power to imagine events into reality. There is no cause for worry until the invalid starts reading science fiction.
[9]Blaine King, "Simak, Master Science-Fiction Writer, Stumbles in Latest Book," *Minneapolis Star*, 3 July 1971: B12.
[10]P. Schuyler Miller, "The Reference Library," *Analog*, December 1971: 165.
[11]Walker, 58.

CHAPTER VI

[1]Angus Wells, ed. *The Best of Clifford D. Simak* (London: Sidgwick and Jackson, 1975): iii.
[2]Walker, 63.
[3]Walker, 61.
[4]Interview with Thomas D. Clareson, Minneapolis, Minnesota, 12 October 1974.
[5]Interview, Clareson.
[6]P. Schuyler Miller, "The Reference Library," *Analog*, June 1972: 168.
[7]Thomas F. Monteleone, *Amazing*, June 1973: 114.
[8]Interview, Clareson.
[9]Fred D. White, *Minneapolis Tribune*, 27 July 1975: D10.
[10]C. N. Manlove, *Science Fiction: Ten Explorations* (Kent, OH: Kent State UP, 1986): 161.
[11]*Trilobite, Dinosaur, and Man: The Earth's Story* (1966) and *Prehistoric Man* (1971), both published by St. Martin's Press.
[12]Clareson, "The Inhabited Universe": 85.

ROBERT J. EWALD

ANNOTATED PRIMARY BIBLIOGRAPHY

NOTE: Items marked with an asterisk [*] have not been personally examined.

NOVELS

All Flesh Is Grass. Garden City, NY: Doubleday & Company, 1965.
Cemetery World. *Analog Science Fiction/Fact,* November 1972-January 1973; New York: G. P. Putnam's Sons, 1973.
A Choice of Gods. New York: G. P. Putnam's Sons, 1972.
City. New York: Gnome Press, 1952. Originally a series of eight short stories, seven published in *Astounding Science Fiction*: "City," May 1944; "Huddling Place," July 1944; "Census," September 1944; "Desertion," November 1944; "Paradise," June 1946; "Hobbies," November 1946; and "Aesop," December 1947. The eighth, "The Trouble with Ants," *Fantastic Adventures,* January 1951, was finally added to the Ace edition of 1981.
The Cosmic Engineers. *Astounding Science Fiction,* February-April 1939; New York: Gnome Press, 1950.
Destiny Doll. As *Reality Doll, Worlds of Fantasy,* Spring 1971; New York: G. P. Putnam's Sons, 1971.
Empire: A Powerful Novel of Intrigue and Action in the Not-So-Distant Future. A Galaxy Science Fiction Novel, No. 7. New York: World Editions, 1951 [paperback]. A reluctant rewrite of an earlier novel by John W. Campbell at Campbell's request.
The Enchanted Pilgrimage. New York: Berkley Publishing Corp./G. P. Putnam's Sons, 1975.
The Fellowship of the Talisman. New York: A Del Rey Book, Ballantine Books, 1978.

134

The Goblin Reservation. Galaxy Science Fiction, April-June 1968; New York: G. P. Putnam's Sons, 1968.

A Heritage of Stars. New York: Berkley Publishing Corp./G. P. Putnam's Sons, 1977.

Highway of Eternity. New York: A Del Rey Book, Ballantine Books, 1986.

Mastodonia. New York: A Del Rey Book, Ballantine Books, 1978. The British title is *Catface.*

Our Children's Children. Worlds of If, June-August 1973; New York: G. P. Putnam's Sons, 1974.

Out of Their Minds. New York: G. P. Putnam's Sons, 1970.

Project Pope. New York: A Del Rey Book, Ballantine Books, 1981.

Ring Around the Sun. Galaxy Science Fiction, December 1952-February 1953; New York: Simon & Schuster, 1953.

Shakespeare's Planet. New York: Berkley Publishing Corp./G. P. Putnam's Sons, 1976.

Special Deliverance. New York: A Del Rey Book, Ballantine Books, 1982.

They Walked Like Men. Garden City, NY: Doubleday, 1962.

Time and Again. As *Time Quarry, Galaxy Science Fiction,* October-December 1950; New York: Simon and Schuster, 1951. Its first paperback publication (New York: Dell Books, 1953) used the title, *First He Died.*

Time Is the Simplest Thing. As *The Fisherman, Analog Science Fiction/Science Fact,* April-July 1961; Garden City, NY: Doubleday, 1961.

The Visitors. Analog Science Fiction/Science Fact, October-December 1979; New York: A Del Rey Book, Ballantine Books, 1979.

Way Station. As *Here Gather the Stars, Galaxy Science Fiction,* June-August 1963; Garden City, NY: Doubleday, 1963.

The Werewolf Principle. New York: G. P. Putnam's Sons, 1967.

Where the Evil Dwells. New York: A Del Rey Book, Ballantine Books, 1982.

Why Call Them Back from Heaven? Garden City, NY: Doubleday, 1967.

SELECTED SHORTER WORKS AND ANTHOLOGIES

All the Traps of Earth and Other Stories. Garden City, NY: Doubleday, 1962. Includes nine of Simak's stories from the late fifties and early sixties: "All the Traps of Earth," 1960; "Goodnight Mr. James," 1951; "Drop Dead," 1956; "No Life of Their Own," 1959; The Sitters," 1958; "Crying Jag," 1960; "Installment Plan," 1959; "Condition of Employment," 1960; "Project Mastodon," 1955.
"The Autumn Land." *The Magazine of Fantasy & Science Fiction* (October 1971): 5-23. 1972 Hugo nominee.
The Best of Clifford D. Simak. Ed. Angus Wells. London: Sidgwick and Jackson, 1975. With an introduction by Clifford D. Simak and a bibliography by Aardvark House. A British selection of ten stories spanning Simak's career from 1939 to 1971, including: "Madness from Mars," 1939; "Sunspot Purge," 1940; "The Sitters," 1958; "A Death in the House," 1959; "Final Gentleman," 1960; "Shotgun Cure," 1961; "Day of Truce," 1963; "Small Deer," 1965; "The Thing in the Stone," 1970; "The Autumn Land," 1971.
Best Science Fiction Stories of Clifford [D.] Simak. London: Faber and Faber, 1967. A British selection of seven short stories from the late fifties and early sixties including "Founding Father," 1957; "Immigrant," 1954; "New Folks Home," 1963; "Crying Jag," 1960; "All the Traps of Earth," 1960; "Lulu," 1957; "Neighbor," 1954.
"The Big Front Yard." *Astounding Science Fiction* (October 1958): 6-49. 1959 Hugo winner for Best Novelette.
*Brother and Other Stories. Ed. by Francis Lyall. England: Severn House, 1986. A collection of Simak's newer stories published in England. Information taken from July 1987 *Locus*.
"Construction Shack." *Worlds of If* (February 1973): 69-81. 1974 Hugo nominee.
"The Creator." *Marvel Tales* (March/April 1935): 129-156. Los Angeles: A Crawford Publication, 1946. A special

commemorative edition was published (San Francisco: Locus Press, 1981) to commemorate Simak's fiftieth year as a science-fiction writer and his recognition as Guest of Honor at the 39th Worldcon at Denver, 1981.

"Epilog." In *Astounding: John W. Campbell Memorial Anthology*. Ed. by Harry Harrison. New York: Random House, 1973, p. 259-274. A ninth "City" story written to commemorate the death of John W. Campbell, now included as an Epilog section in the most recent paperback reprints of *City*.

"Grotto of the Dancing Deer." *Analog Science Fiction/Science Fact* (April 1980): 144-159. 1981 Hugo and Nebula award winner for Best Short Story.

"The Marathon Photograph." In *Threads of Time: Three Original Novellas of Science Fiction*, ed. by Robert Silverberg. Nashville, TN: Thomas Nelson Inc., 1974, p. 95-151. One of Simak's better novellas, frequently overlooked by critics.

Nebula Award Stories, No. 6. Garden City, New York: Doubleday, 1971. Only fiction anthology ever edited by Simak.

"Rule 18." *Astounding Science Fiction* (July 1938): 32-51. Simak's first story published by John W. Campbell.

Skirmish: The Great Short Fiction of Clifford D. Simak. New York: G. P. Putnam's Sons, 1977. Another career-spanning anthology of ten short stories from the forties to the seventies including "Huddling Place," 1944; "Desertion," 1944; "Skirmish," 1950; "Good Night, Mr. James," 1951; "The Sitters," 1958; "The Big Front Yard," 1958; "All the Traps of Earth," 1960; "The Thing in the Stone," 1970; "The Autumn Land," 1971; "The Ghost of a Model T," 1975.

So Bright the Vision. New York: Ace, 1968. A paperback collection of four late fifties and early sixties novelettes, all alien encounter themes, including "The Golden Bugs," 1960; "Leg. Forst," 1958; "So Bright the Vision," 1954; "Galactic Chest," 1956.

Strangers in the Universe. New York: Simon and Schuster, 1956. Simak's first hardcover anthology of eleven short stories, all from the fifties, including "Shadow Show,"

1953; "Contraption," 1953; "The Answers," 1953; "The Fence," 1953; "Beachhead," 1951; "Kindergarten," 1953; "Mirage," 1956; "Skirmish," 1950; "Retrograde Evolution," 1953; "Immigrant," 1954.

"The Street That Wasn't There." *Comet Stories* (July 1941): 18-27. One of Simak's rare collaborations—with horror writer Carl Jacobi.

"The Thing in the Stone." *Worlds of If* (March 1970): 30-70,152. 1971 Hugo 2nd Best Novella and Nebula Runner-Up for Best Novella.

The Trouble with Tycho. Amazing Stories (October 1960): 8-67. New York: Ace, 1961.

"Unsilent Spring." In *Stellar No. 2: Science Fiction Stories*, ed. by Judy-Lynn del Rey. New York: Ballantine Books, 1976, 168-209 [paper]. Notable only as Simak's only collaboration with his son Richard.

The Worlds of Clifford Simak. New York: Simon and Schuster, 1960. London: Faber and Faber, 1961 as *Aliens for Neighbours: Science Fiction Stories.* Twelve of Simak's best short stories from the fifties including "Dusty Zebra," 1954; "Honorable Opponent," 1956; "Carbon Copy," 1957; "Founding Father," 1957; "Idiot's Crusade," 1954; "The Big Front Yard," 1958; "Operation Stinky," 1957; "Jackpot," 1956; "Death Scene," 1957; "Green Thumb," 1954; "Lulu," 1957; "Neighbor," 1954.

"The World of the Red Sun." *Wonder Stories* (December 1931): 878-889. Simak's first published story.

Worlds Without End. New York: Belmont, 1964 [paper]. Contains three novelettes from the mid-fifties: "Worlds Without End," 1956; "The Spaceman's Van Gogh," 1956; "Full Cycle," 1955.

DRAMATIC PRESENTATIONS

"Courtesy." *Dimension X.* NBC. 19 November 1950. Adapted from the story "Courtesy," 1951.

"Drop Dead." *X Minus One.* NBC. 22 August 1957. Adapted from the story "Drop Dead," 1956.

"How to 'Do It Yourself' of the Twenty-First Century." *X Minus One*. NBC. 3 April 1956. Adapted from the story "How-2," 1954.

How to Make a Man. Adapted for the theatre by William Welch from the story "How-2," 1954, and directed by Eddie Bracken. The cast included Tommy Noonan, Barbara Britton, and Peter Marshall, and the first performance was held at the Cass Theatre, Detroit, Michigan on December 26, 1960.

NON-FICTION

NOTE: Because of Simak's long journalistic career and extensive science writing, Simak's non-fiction listings here are severely limited. For a more complete listing of Simak's non-fiction, see Muriel Becker's *Clifford D. Simak: A Primary and Secondary Bibliography* (Boston: G. K. Hall, 1980).

"The Face of Science Fiction." *Minnesota Libraries* (September 1953): 197-201. Simak informally discusses science fiction, his early interest in Verne, Haggard, and Wells, and the demands science fiction makes on the writer.

"Foreword." In *Skirmish: The Great Short Fiction of Clifford D. Simak* (New York: G. P. Putnam's Sons, 1977), p. 7-12. After describing the stories, Simak discusses pastoralism, the use of robots, and his general tone of optimism.

From Atoms to Infinity: Readings in Modern Science. New York: Harper & Row, 1965. A collection of science essays edited by Simak.

"Introduction." In *The Best of Clifford D. Simak.* Ed. by Angus Wells (London: Sidgwick and Jackson, 1975), 7-12. Simak writes of his own writing, how his roots affected his work, and his general philosophy of life.

"Jenkins Would Be Proud." *Algol: The Magazine about Science Fiction* (Summer-Fall 1977): 9-10, 12-13. Simak's "Grand Master" keynote speech at the 1977 Nebula Awards Banquet, New York, 30 April.

The March of Science. New York: Harper & Row, 1971. Thirty-seven articles on modern science by ten writers, including Nourse, Silverberg, Asimov, and Ley.

Prehistoric Man. New York: St. Martin's Press, 1971. Simak's treatment of early humans sees them as already human rather than vicious or animalistic.

"Room Enough for All of Us." *Extrapolation* (May 1972): 102-105. The text of Simak's speech at Noreascon (the World Science Fiction Convention in Boston on September 5, 1971). Simak is very optimistic about the future of science fiction, and chides at the "shallowness of the controversy" going on among critics, fans, and academics.

Trilobite, Dinosaur, and Man: The Earth's Story. New York: St. Martin's Press, 1966. Simak gives an overview of geological history until the coming of intelligence.

*"Where's Hawk Carse!" *Ad Astra* [fanzine] (July 1939): 3-5. Simak declares his early views on how science fiction should be written: better characterization, humor, and more human interest.

Wonder and Glory: The Story of the Universe. New York: St. Martin's Press, 1969. Simak presents various theories of the origin of the universe and speculates on life and intelligence in the universe.

FILM

A Career in Science Fiction: An Interview with Clifford Simak. Lawrence: University of Kansas, 1975. James Gunn, Interviewer. The Literature of Science Fiction Film Lecture Series. Simak discusses the evolution of his writing and writers who have influenced him.

ANNOTATED SECONDARY
BIBLIOGRAPHY

NOTE: Items marked with an asterisk [*] have not been personally examined.

Aldiss, Brian. *Billion Year Spree: The True History of Science Fiction.* Garden City, NY: Doubleday, 1973, p. 234-235, 246, 249. Revised as *Trillion Year Spree: The History of Science Fiction* with David Wingrove. New York: Atheneum, 1986. Aldiss categorizes *City* as an example of the doomsday story and "the research lab approach" used by Campbell in *Astounding* in the forties, and describes Simak's *Astounding* aliens as "generally just men without sin."

Amis, Kingsley. *New Maps of Hell: A Survey of Science Fiction.* New York: Harcourt Brace, 1960. Amis was the first British critic to recognize Simak's pastoralism and uses "The Big Front Yard" as an example of Simak's assertion of the rights of the individual against the "forces of convention and authority."

Asimov, Isaac. *In Memory Yet Green: The Autobiography of Isaac Asimov, 1920-1954.* New York: Avon Books, 1979. Asimov notes his early contacts with Simak and Simak's influence on his style.

Bailey, J. O. *Pilgrims through Space and Time: Trends and Patterns in Scientific and Utopian Fiction.* New York: Argus, 1947; rpt. Westport, CT: Greenwood, 1972. Bailey feels "The Creator" is clearly derived from Stapledon's *Star Maker*; such treatment, though brief, is significant as Bailey refers to few pulp writers in this seminal work.

Becker, Muriel R. *Clifford D. Simak: A Primary and Secondary Bibliography. Masters of Science Fiction and Fan-*

tasy. Ed. by L. W. Currey. Boston: G. K. Hall, 1980. An invaluable work to the Simak scholar, the most complete, error-free comprehensive bibliography of Simak's fiction, non-fiction, media, and criticism (Becker even lists Simak's westerns and air stories). The excellent introduction includes an interview with Simak containing biographical information not given to anyone since Moskowitz.

Carter, Paul A. *The Creation of Tomorrow: 50 Years of Magazine Science Fiction.* New York: Columbia UP, 1977. One of the very few studies which deals with Simak's early magazine short fiction: "Hermit of Mars," "Tools," and "The Street That Wasn't There."

Chapman, Edgar L. *"The Fellowship of the Talisman."* In *Survey of Modern Fantasy Literature.* Ed. by Frank N. Magill. Englewood Cliffs, NJ: Salem Press, 1983, Vol. II, p. 549-552. Places novel in Tolkien-Lewis tradition, though second-rate. Praises Simak's plotting and characterization, but his "whimsy and gentle humor grow tiresome."

Clareson, Thomas D. *"City."* In *Survey of Science Fiction Literature.* Ed. by Frank N. Magill. Englewood Cliffs, NJ: Salem Press, 1979, Vol. I, p. 369-37. Well-polished plot summaries of each episode.

_____. "Clifford D. Simak." In *Twentieth Century American Science-Fiction Writers* (Dictionary of Literary Biography, Vol. 8). Ed. David Cowart and Thomas L. Wymer. Detroit: Gale, 1981, Part 2: M-Z, p. 119-127. One of the best and most detailed analyses of Simak's fiction, including some keen insights into the thematic connections between *City, A Choice of Gods,* and *A Heritage of Stars,* Simak's pastoralism and quest for religious affirmation, and a brief discussion of Simak's fantasy not found elsewhere.

_____. "Clifford D. Simak: The Inhabited Universe." In *Voices for the Future: Essays on Major Science Fiction Writers.* Ed. by Thomas D. Clareson. Bowling Green, OH: Bowling Green University Popular Press, 1976, p. 64-87, 265-267. The first comprehensive study of Simak's work from the publication of Simak's first story,

"The World of the Red Sun" (1931) to *A Choice of Gods* (1972). Considering most of Simak's memorable works during this period, especially a number of early stories before *City*, Clareson defines the major themes associated with Simak: the denunciation of technological society, the brotherhood of intelligent life, and the mechanistic, uncaring Principle. Clareson finds *City* a milestone in its "condemnation of man's surrender to technology," freeing science fiction from established patterns and giving the genre a "moral stature." Clareson also makes a valuable contribution by highlighting certain characteristic literary devices and techniques used frequently by Simak: the newspaperman hero, the concept of parallel worlds, the pastoral quality, and the Millville setting.

_____. "Many Futures, Many Worlds." In *Many Futures, Many Worlds: Theme and Form in Science Fiction.* Ed. by Thomas D. Clareson. Kent, OH: Kent State UP, 1977, p. 14-25. Clareson mentions Stapledon's "mystic, transcendental" influence on Simak and other writers, citing "Desertion" as an early example of the "exploration of inner space" found in much more recent writing.

de Camp, L. Sprague. *Science Fiction Handbook: The Writing of Imaginative Fiction.* New York: Hermitage House, 1953; rpt. as *Science Fiction Handbook, Revised,* Philadelphia: Owlswick Press, 1975; New York: McGraw Hill, 1977. Original edition contains rare biographical sketch of Simak and compares Simak's style to Asimov's and his plots to van Vogt's (reprints omit this biographical information and criticism).

Goldin, Stephen. "*Way Station.*" In *Survey of Science Fiction Literature.* Ed. by Frank N. Magill. Englewood Cliffs, NJ: Salem, 1979, Vol. 5, p. 2429-2432. Rpt. in *Science Fiction Alien Encounter.* Ed. by Frank N. Magill. Pasadena, CA: Salem Softbacks, 1981. An excellent discussion centering the conflict in the novel on the character of Enoch Wallace.

Gunn, James. *Alternate Worlds: The Illustrated History of Science Fiction.* Englewood Cliffs, NJ: Prentice-Hall, 1975. In Chapter Twelve, Gunn analyzes Simak's flexibility to write for new and varied markets like *The Maga-*

zine of Fantasy & Science Fiction and *Galaxy*, even though Simak was identified with Campbell's *Astounding* stable.

Lomax, William. "The Invisible 'Alien' in the Science Fiction of Clifford Simak." *Extrapolation* 30:2 (Summer 1989): 133-145. Lomax perceives the alien encounter as a "paradigm of both human weakness and human potential," demonstrating Simak's unique narrative strategy which generates a role reversal of identities between human and alien. Inside the "clown costumes" of his aliens are human minds and Simak forces us to define our humanity by setting it over against alienness.

Lundwall, Sam J. *Science Fiction: What It's All About.* New York: Ace, 1971. Lundwall notes Simak's reversal of traditional roles of robots and androids in such novels as *City, Time and Again,* and *The Werewolf Principle.*

Manlove, C. N. *Science Fiction: Ten Explorations.* Kent, OH: The Kent State UP, 1986. Manlove chooses *Shakespeare's Planet* as a touchstone work to discuss Simak's symbolic use of aliens. In addition, Manlove includes some intriguing, but shaky, speculations on Simak's use of structure and language for symbolic purposes.

Moskowitz, Sam. "S F Profile: The Saintly Heresy of Clifford D. Simak." *Amazing Stories* (June 1962): 86-97. Rpt. "Clifford D. Simak." In *Seekers of Tomorrow: Masters of Modern Science Fiction.* Cleveland: World Publishing Co., 1966, p. 266-282; New York: Ballantine, 1967. Until Muriel Becker's bibliography, the most accurate bio-bibliographical profile of Simak's life and works through 1964, one to which Simak always refers the critic when biographical questions are asked in an interview. Rich in details about Simak's early life and writing (over thirty short stories and novels are cited) and high in praise for Simak's art as a science fiction writer.

_____. "Religion in Science Fiction: God, Space, and Faith." *Amazing Stories* (April 1965): 87-99. Rpt. as part of *Strange Horizons: The Spectrum of Science Fiction.* New York: Charles Scribner's Sons, 1976, p. 11-12, 117. Comments on Simak's use of religion in his science fiction, especially in his earlier work. Calls "The Creator"

When the Fires Burn High and the Wind Is from the North

the first "sacrilegious" SF story and discusses "The Voice in the Void," *The Cosmic Engineers*, "Hunch," and *Time and Again*.

*Owings, Mark. "The Electric Bibliograph." *The WSFA Journal* (April-May 1969): 29-32. Rpt. in pamphlet form Baltimore, MD: Alice & Jay Haldeman, 1971. The first bibliography of Simak's works.

Pascoe, Jason. "Clifford Simak: The Compassionate Universe." *Winding Numbers* (Summer 1977): 22-26. Pascoe develops the idea that a number of Simak's short stories and novellas of the fifties are pessimistic, but move towards optimism by 1958. Includes a selected bibliography of forty-six items.

Pringle, David. "Aliens for Neighbours: A Reassessment of Clifford D. Simak." *Foundation: The Review of Science Fiction* (March 1977): 15-29. A very perceptive but acid-tinged assessment from a British critic. Pringle begins by stressing Simak's old age as a factor in his writing in a field where most authors are young. Second, Pringle finds Simak's works repetitive, obsessive, and lacking in ideas, and he attributes Simak's success to readers who prefer moral seriousness and cozy sentimentalism to "mind-blowing" ideas. Pringle then isolates twelve themes from Simak's fiction and cites appropriate stories to illustrate each theme: (1) The Old Man; (2) The House; (3) Listening to the Stars; (4) The Neighbour; (5) The Alien; (6) The Pastoral; (7) Animals; (8) The Evils of the City; (9) Servants; (10) The Frontier; (11) Bartering; (12) The Artifact.

Rogers, Alva. *A Requiem for Astounding*. Chicago: Advent, 1964. Rogers is one of the very few critical sources on Simak's early work—he comments on seventeen of the twenty-nine stories published in *Astounding*, including *The Cosmic Engineers*.

Schweitzer, Darrell. "Clifford Simak." In *Science Fiction Voices #5*. Ed. by Darrell Schweitzer. San Bernardino, CA: Borgo Press, 1981, p. 48-55. An interview with Simak, significant for Simak's revelations of his writing methods and some penetrating comments on adaptations of his work to the media.

145

Stableford, Brian. "*Ring Around the Sun.*" In *Survey of Science Fiction Literature.* Ed. by Frank N. Magill. Englewood Cliffs, NJ: Salem Press, 1979, Vol. 4, 1794-1798. Sharply criticizes the novel for its "sickly" sentimentalism and its simplistic message "insulting or at least patronizing to readers." The strengths of the novel lie in the emotional involvement with the hero as his real nature is revealed and the novel's concerns for what were real anxieties in the 1950s.

Tweet, Roald D. "Clifford D. Simak: 1904- ." In *Science Fiction Writers: Critical Studies of the Major Authors from the Early Nineteenth Century to the Present Day.* Ed. by E. F. Bleiler. New York: Scribner's, 1982, p. 513-518. An excellent overview of Simak's major works, including significant stories like "A Death in the House" and "All the Traps of Earth." Tweet defines Simak's pastoralism as "an ideal social structure for neighborliness," and notes that critics often overlook Simak as too "pastoral" and "religiously conservative." He feels Simak has declined in the 1960s and '70s, but returned to form with *The Visitors.*

Walker, Paul. "Clifford Simak: An Interview." *Luna Monthly* (Spring 1975): 1-6. Rpt. in *Speaking of Science Fiction.* Oradell, NJ: Luna Publications, 1978, p. 56-67. An in-depth interview in which Simak answers questions about mixing fantasy and science fiction, his "mysticism," the purpose of life and intelligence, religion, man and technology, regionalism, and his pessimism and/or optimism.

Weinkauf, Mary S. "Simak, Clifford D(onald)." In *Twentieth Century Science-Fiction Writers.* Ed. by Curtis C. Smith. 2nd edition. Chicago: St. James, 1986, p. 666-668. A very broad-brush and slyly cynical overview of Simak's works, barely touching on his major themes. A tragic oversight—Muriel Becker's complete bibliography is missing from the critical apparatus.

White, George. "His World is Limited Only by Boundaries of Imagination." *Minneapolis Tribune* (26 August 1976): Sect. C, p. 1, 6. Honors Simak on his retirement, integrating Simak's many achievements in both journalism and science fiction writing, and presenting highlights on Simak's life and career by people who knew him personally. Wollheim, Donald A. "Towards Galactic Maturity." *The Universe Makers: Science Fiction Today.* New York: Harper & Row, 1971, p. 90-93. Devotes Chapter 29 to Simak and his works. Wollheim notes that Simak, surrounded in his office by depressing news bulletins, is still able to "reflect...a sense of the joy of life."

INDEX

When the Fires Burn High and the Wind Is from the North

ABOUT ROBERT J. EWALD

ROBERT J. EWALD is Professor Emeritus of English from a small Midwestern college, the University of Findlay, in Findlay, Ohio. He has been reading science fiction since he was ten years old, which makes him a fan of over sixty-five years. For part of his life, Ewald programmed computers for various businesses until he embarked on a second career as an English teacher. Ewald has published numerous book reviews, and was a recent contributor to the Tymn and Ashley encyclopedia of science fiction, fantasy, and weird fiction magazines. This is his first published book.

Milton Keynes UK
Ingram Content Group UK Ltd.
UKHW021851211024
450061UK00005B/22